What People Are Saying

"We can all point to mentors who have had an outsized impact on our careers, but how do you actually find one and build a productive relationship? Michelle Estades Jack takes the guesswork out of the process with this practical step-by-step guide. She provides questions for reflection that provide the mentee with a richer experience while finding an inspiring mentor."

–Kari Durham, Senior Vice President Human Resources, Skyworks Solutions Inc.

"*The ABC Playbook for the Ultimate Mentee Experience* is an indispensable tool for anyone seeking to deepen their understanding of mentorship and harness its full potential for personal and professional growth.

"It provides a thoughtful framework for mentees to reflect on their goals, initiate a meaningful dialogue with mentors, and engage in a transformative learning process.

"Whether you're embarking on a new mentorship relationship or seeking to enhance an existing one, this playbook is a valuable resource. It guides you through a series of reflective activities and strategic planning, encouraging engagement and providing a sense of purpose and direction in your professional journey. Engaging with this playbook is not just about being mentored; it's about embarking on a path of self-discovery and impactful growth."

–Joanna Kostecka, Vice President Cloud Global Supply Chain, Microsoft

"A growing number of experts suggest that people seeking mentorship need to be prepared to receive coaching and wisdom from others, but there are few resources to help with this preparation. *Inspire to Aspire* provides mentees with fantastic worksheets and suggestions to enable people to find a compatible mentor and be ready to learn and progress toward their goals. It will benefit anyone who takes the time to go through it carefully."

–Art Markman, Founding Director of the Human Dimensions of Organizations program at the University of Texas at Austin and author of Bring Your Brain to Work

"Most mentorship programs are drowning in ambiguity and starving for structure. Without a structured approach, it's difficult for both parties to fully maximize their mentorship outcome. *Inspire to Aspire* is the playbook needed to help people achieve their peak potential."

–Mark Bray, President, ACR Supply Company; The 40 Under 40 Leadership Award Recipient, East Carolina University

INSPIRE TO ASPIRE

ABC PLAYBOOK → ← FOR THE ULTIMATE MENTEE EXPERIENCE

MICHELLE ESTADES JACK
WITH **JENNIFER CHLOUPEK, M.Ed.**

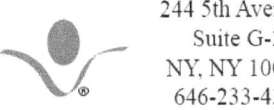

DocUmeant *Publishing*
244 5th Avenue
Suite G-200
NY, NY 10001
646-233-4366
www.DocUmeantPublishing.com

© 2024 All rights reserved. Michelle Estades-Jack & Jennifer Chloupek, M.Ed.

Published by
DocUmeant Publishing
244 5th Avenue, Suite G-200
NY, NY 10001
646–233–4366

Limit of Liability and Disclaimer of Warranty: The publisher has used its best efforts in preparing this book and the information provided herein is provided "as is.

No part of this book may be reproduced or transmitted in any form or by any means, electronic or mechanical, including photocopying, recording or by any information storage or retrieval system, except as may be expressly permitted by law or in writing from the publisher, or except by a reviewer who may quote brief passages in review to be printed in a magazine, newspaper, or online website.

Permission should be addressed in writing to:
publisher@DocUmeantPublishing.com

Edited by Philip S. Marks

Cover Design, Illustrations, and layout by DocUmeant Designs
www.DocUmeantDesigns.com

Library of Congress Cataloging-in-Publication Data

Names: Estades Jack, Michelle, author. | Chloupek, Jennifer, author.
Title: Inspire to aspire : ABC playbook for the ultimate mentor experience / Michelle Estades Jack with Jennifer Chloupek, M.Ed.
Description: NY, NY : DocUmeant Publishing, [2024] | Summary: "Embark on a thrilling odyssey with our Mentee ABC Playbook - Inspire to Aspire for the Ultimate Mentee Experience. Ignite your mentorship journey with this dynamic roadmap that will inspire you. This playbook unveils a roadmap, eliminating the awkward uncertainties of mentorship and offering hands-on guidance to cultivate your aspirational story. Unleash your potential through this strategic approach, maximizing the impact of the most pivotal relationship in your career, your mentor. Seize the mentorship journey crafted to propel you to extraordinary heights with unwavering confidence and purpose, meticulously designed for your aspirations"-- Provided by publisher.
Identifiers: LCCN 2024013457 | ISBN 9781957832319 (paperback)
Subjects: LCSH: Mentoring.
Classification: LCC BF637.M45 E88 2024 | DDC 158.3--dc23/eng/20240506
LC record available at https://lccn.loc.gov/2024013457

To all the mentors
that inspire those that aspire.

Contents

ACKNOWLEDGMENTS   IX

INTRODUCTION   XI

PART 1

CORE AWARENESS: PREPARE FOR THE PARTNERSHIP   1

    Activity 1: Discovery 5

    Activity 2: Core Values 8

    Activity 3: Personal Vision 13

    Discovery Recap 19

    Activity 4: Find Your Mentor. 22

    Activity 5: Chemistry Meeting. 28

PART 2

CORE BEHAVIORS: PERSONAL VIEW   35

    Activity 1: Work and Home Friction 36

    Activity 2: Emotional Intelligence 42

    Activity 3: Getting Out of Your Own Head 44

    Activity 4: Goal Setting. 50

    Activity 5: Career Transition 54

    Activity 6: Visibility and Influence. 62

    Activity 7: Confidence. 69

Activity 8: Risk-taking and Initiative 77

Mid-Term Calibration 81

Reflection and What's Next 83

PART 3

CORE CONNECTIONS: GLOBAL VIEW — 91

Activity 1: Networking 92

Activity 2: Corporate Culture 97

Activity 3: Navigating Corporate Politics. 100

Activity 4: Allyships 103

Partnership Sunset and Final Calibration. 113

ADDITIONAL RESOURCES

Proposed Timeline 117

Mentorship Tracker. 119

MEET THE AUTHORS — 149

Acknowledgments

I would like to express my deepest gratitude to the numerous mentors who have played an instrumental role in shaping my career and providing invaluable guidance and support throughout the process of writing this book. Their unwavering commitment to impart knowledge and expertise has been a beacon of inspiration, illuminating the path toward success.

Special thank you to Kari Durham, an incredible mentor and friend, who provided constructive feedback, insightful advice, and indispensable suggestions. She continues to inspire and support others through her everlasting allyship.

I am profoundly grateful for the patience and wisdom Jennifer Chloupek, my coauthor, provided, who guided me through the complexities of the writing process and offered unwavering encouragement. I am eternally grateful to Ginger Marks, our publisher, as her patience and guidance created a path to write a book, a lifelong dream of mine.

I am sincerely grateful for the contributions of Mark Fleischhauer who challenged the process to make it better and more creative.

Finally, I am grateful for all of the wonderful mentors that continue to guide and foster me. Your mentorship has not only enriched this book but has also left an enduring impact on my personal and professional development. I am truly fortunate to have had the privilege of learning from each of you.

May we all have mentors that unselfishly give both their wisdom and time.

This book stands as a testament to the collective wisdom and generosity of those who have invested in my journey. Thank you for being beacons of guidance, for sharing your expertise, and for being an integral part of my growth as a writer and individual. Your impact on this project is immeasurable, and I am sincerely grateful for your enduring support.

Introduction

Welcome to the ABC Playbook. This playbook is designed for the ultimate mentee/mentor experience. In this playbook, you will find a variety of activities, discoveries, and revelations to help you gain a deeper understanding of yourself, prioritize what you really want, and guide your focus on your aspirations. You will also find a proposed timeline to guide you through the experience with a defined beginning and end. And to keep you on track, Mentorship Tracker and midterm and final calibration tools are included. This playbook is designed to maximize both you and your mentor's time and energy.

This playbook has a companion handbook, *Aspire to Inspire*. The *Aspire to Inspire* handbook guides the mentor through your program with sections that mirror your playbook. These books are intended to work in conjunction with each other.

Purpose

When you aspire to do more in your professional career, a mentor program may be the opportunity to find inspiration from a more seasoned leader. A seasoned leader who has experience in the areas that you aspire to achieve such as managing individuals and groups, global responsibility, multi-site control, mergers, system transformations, processes, and markets. Someone who has the scars that only experience can bring and is willing to guide you, challenge you, and inspire you on a path not yet known to you.

Maybe you have worked with a mentor before, but it was clunky and awkward. Or perhaps it was a great experience. Sometimes this can get tricky as you have questions and are not sure how to ask them. On the flip side, a mentor wants to help, and has agreed to help, but needs you to tell them **HOW** they can help. This playbook provides the framework to enjoy a mutually beneficial relationship with your mentor and ensure that both of you are satisfied with the results.

Understand

Let us take this opportunity to understand the difference between a mentor, a coach, and a sponsor. This will help you understand if a mentor is really what you need.

A mentor is a trusted advisor who guides the mentee. Mentors serve as beacons, guiding the mentee through the intricate paths of personal and professional growth. Mentors offer guidance based on experiences they have had in their careers as they are usually senior to the mentee. A mentor stands as a leader in their field and imparts not only practical knowledge but also instills the qualities of visionary and thought leadership. They become mentors who do not just teach skills but inspire mentees to cultivate their unique leadership styles, fostering the emergence of future leaders. The mentor/mentee relationship becomes a transformative journey, leaving an enduring imprint on the mentee's life trajectory. The mentee/mentor relationship is based on trust, aligned values, commitment, and mutual respect.

A coach is engaged by you or your organization to focus on behaviors and perhaps skills that are hindering their client. Coaches focus on performance, personal and/or professional growth, and usually have specific areas of expertise. The coach provides tools based on the needs of the client to achieve the client's aspirations. The focus is usually targeted and may focus on areas of development such as communication, decision-making, prioritization, managing conflict, and other non-technical skills. The relationship is usually for a specified period with a specified end goal that is funded by either their client or the client's organization.

A sponsor is a senior-level advocate who actively supports the mentee's advancement. They use their influence to provide opportunities and visibility for the mentees. The focus of the sponsor is to help the mentee advance their career by recommending them for projects and opportunities that provide visibility, and promotions. A sponsor could be a manager or a person with a higher-level position with influence.

This program is based on experiences of the authors and is in no way to be considered therapy. A mentor, coach, or sponsor does provide guidance, support, or advice; however, they do not provide counseling that is or can be perceived as therapy.

Therapy

As more organizations focus on mental health in the workplace, it is important to understand the difference between mentorship and therapy. Therapy is a professional relationship between a licensed mental health professional, i.e., therapist, and client that focuses on emotional, psychological, or behavioral issues that cause distress or impairment of the client's life. Signs that a therapist may be more appropriate could be if the mentee shows signs of persistent emotional distress, difficulties coping with life changes, unhealthy coping mechanisms, trauma, chronic physical symptoms, or is consistently overwhelmed or stressed.

Now that we have defined these roles, based on your aspirations, which role most aligns with your aspirations. How do you know?

....

....

....

....

....

Playbook Overview

There are three sections in this book and an additional resource section. The main three sections are: A core Awareness, B core Behaviors, and C core Connections.

You will begin with core Awareness as you prepare for the partnership. In this section, you will embark on a personal discovery and prioritize the work with your mentor. Then you dive deeply into your values with reflective questions that reveal your values and how they impact your aspirations. Then you curate your personal vision to provide clarity as you launch your aspirational journey with your mentor.

After you have completed your discovery and are ready to find your mentor, the Find Your Mentor section guides you. This section defines characteristics of mentors, and, in turn, you will define what characteristics inspire you. Finally, you are ready to meet your mentor and have the all-important chemistry meeting. This meeting is the launching pad for the future partnership where expectations and rules of engagement are defined and agreed upon.

Core Behaviors is where your work begins from your Personal View Discovery where you will select three to four core Behaviors. Your prioritized three to four core Behaviors become the topic of individual mentor sessions. No matter which areas you prioritize, explanations and guided questions are provided to reveal an awareness of yourself and discovery opportunities to reveal to your mentor.

Each activity in core Behaviors is self-reflective and includes questions and tools that guide you. At the conclusion of each core Behavior, a reality reveal section and a suggested question for your mentor is provided. The reality reveal sections are designated areas for you to document what "ahas" or "gems" you found during the exercise, questions, or insights. The suggested question is just a suggestion; however, you can choose to ask a different question or just discuss your responses to the exercise with your mentor. This section will be three to four sessions depending on how many Behaviors you decide to focus on. Each of these Behaviors will be a stand-alone session with your mentor.

Before you launch into the final section, core Connections, a midterm calibration tool is provided to ensure alignment with your aspirations and expectations.

The final section, core Connections, is when you reflect on the work, four global topics are revealed where you will select one to two topics based on your Global View Discovery section in core Awareness, next steps, final calibration, and partnership sunset. This section will be three to four sessions depending on number of global topics.

It is recommended that your mentorship sessions occur every two weeks to allow time for the activities and reflection.

The Additional Resources section includes a **"Proposed Timeline" on page 117** and **Mentee Tracker Pages** to summarize inspirations, note new material, and a timeout-reveal to help you get to know each other better on a personal level.

Part 1

Core Awareness: Prepare for the Partnership

Activity 1: Discovery
Activity 2: Core Values
Activity 3: Personal Vision
Discovery Recap
Activity 4: Find Your Mentor
Activity 5: Chemistry Meeting

CORE AWARENESS
Prepare for the Partnership

To prepare for the partnership, it is important for you to understand the role you want the mentor to play, benefits of a mentor, goals and how you envision success. This is a brief introduction as you prepare to embark on your mentorship journey.

Think about the questions below as you prepare for your mentor/mentee partnership.

As you think about a potential mentor, are you seeking someone who has certain accomplishments? Examples could be a person who has managed their career and family successfully or someone who has incredible loyalty from their team. Maybe you are inspired by someone who fosters an environment where ideas flourish and innovations thrive or has "been there and done that." Perhaps it is someone who is more direct or who can tell you the harsh truths or weaves a story around what is possible.

What sort of mentor would inspire you?

....
....
....
....
....
....
....
....

You have decided that perhaps a mentor is what you need to achieve your aspirations. Perhaps you have heard from colleagues who have achieved greater heights through mentorship. When you think of a mentor, how can a mentor inspire you? What would be the benefit of a mentor?

As you think about a mentorship program, what are your aspirations with a mentor? Can you express these aspirations in three simple sentences?

The mentorship program is an intensive program that involves time and energy. The success is defined by the work performed by you. By the end of this program, how will you define success?

Part 1: Core Awareness: Prepare for the Partnership

⟫ Activity 1: Discovery

This activity will help you identify where you see your greatest need for a mentor. You will complete the self-assessment and reflect on the results to gain a deeper understanding of your needs.

This discovery assessment is organized into two areas, the personal awareness view, and the global awareness view. Personal view is intrinsic and personal to you. Global view is more extrinsic and externally focused. For the partnership, select three to four from the personal view section and one to two in the global awareness section.

Prioritize by circling your response.

PERSONAL VIEW DISCOVERY

1. **Work and Home Friction**: How important is it for you to balance work and home with competing demands on your time, energy, and space?

   High Priority   Somewhat a Priority   Not a Priority

2. **Emotional Intelligence:** How important is it for you to develop awareness and tools to recognize an emotional response vs. curiosity and compassion?

   High Priority   Somewhat a Priority   Not a Priority

3. **Getting Out of Your Own Head:** Sometimes we just cannot get where we want to go due to overthinking, fear, and/or self-doubt. It is important for you to understand what is holding you back from achieving your goals.

   High Priority   Somewhat a Priority   Not a Priority

4. **Goal Setting:** Is goal setting a challenge? How important is it for you to set clear, achievable goals, create action plans and actually achieve those goals?

   High Priority   Somewhat a Priority   Not a Priority

5. Career Transitions: You may be in a career transition or even considering a transition. This can be very challenging and intimidating. How important is it for you to receive guidance on a potential role, a new role, or a role transition?

High Priority   Somewhat a Priority   Not a Priority

6. Visibility and Influence: When you think of the level of visibility you have and the influence that you have, how important is it for you to focus on increasing visibility and influence?

High Priority   Somewhat a Priority   Not a Priority

7. Confidence: How important is self-confidence to your aspirations?

High Priority   Somewhat a Priority   Not a Priority

8. Risk Taking and Initiative: How important is it for you to have a mentor who challenges you to take risks and initiatives to expand outside of your comfort zone?

High Priority   Somewhat a Priority   Not a Priority

GLOBAL VIEW DISCOVERY

1. Networking: How important is it for you to expand your professional network and build meaningful relationships in your industry?

High Priority   Somewhat a Priority   Not a Priority

2. Organizational Culture: How important is it for you to identify, understand and navigate organizational culture?

High Priority   Somewhat a Priority   Not a Priority

3. Navigating Corporate Politics: Most organizations have politics. How important is it for you to know how things get done, who to interface with on important topics and how to navigate difficulties?

High Priority   Somewhat a Priority   Not a Priority

4. Allyships: Allies play a pivotal role in shaping organizational culture, driving innovation, and fostering a workplace where every individual feels valued and empowered to contribute their best. How important is it for you to understand the importance of allyship, how to expand your allyships and become a better ally?

High Priority   Somewhat a Priority   Not a Priority

Once you have completed your discovery, review your ratings to identify the areas that align with your aspirations so that you prioritize those with your mentor. For the ultimate mentor experience, prioritize 3 to 4 in the personal view section and 1 to 3 in the global view section. This will enable you and your mentor focus on the areas that matter most to your aspirations.

Reality reveal sections in this playbook provide space where you can pause, think, and reflect. This area is a space for you to reveal what you have learned, how you can apply your learning, and how your actions today may or may not allow you to achieve your goals. It also is a space for you to reflect on what is getting in your way, "Aha's, gems, thoughts, questions, and next steps.

Reality Reveal

....

....

....

....

....

....

》》 Activity 2: Core Values

Your core values are your standards that are unique and intrinsic to you. They guide how you view the world and what inspires you. By identifying your core values, you gain insights into why things, situations, and relationships are more or less important, more or less exciting, or more or less frightening to you. It also gives you an understanding that with our uniqueness, not everyone has the same values or even the same definition, which can lead to unintended conflicts and misunderstandings.

This activity will help you identify your core values. You will review your core values and consider how these values influence what is important to you. As you go through these values, there may be some that you aspire to; however, it is imperative that you identify your true values. At the end, you will assess how they show up in your life and work. You may even want to look up the definition of the value to see if that definition aligns with your value as defined and experienced by you.

Also, when you compare values with other individuals you may notice that their definition of that value may be different than your own. When you meet with your mentor, compare values, and learn how your values and theirs align or differ. How are these values revealed in your and your mentor's personal and professional lives?

Below you will find a list of values. Be honest with yourself and rate each value based on the authentic you vs. the aspirational you. If your value is missing, there is space provided at the bottom of the table.

If you rate them all high or low, review again and narrow your selections to 4.

Rate each value on a scale from 1 to 5. 1 - not important and 5 - must haves

Value	Rating	Value	Rating
Achievement		Balance	
Adventure		Happiness	
Creativity		Health	
Courage		Peace	
Curiosity		Learning	
Growth		Self-discipline	
Authenticity		Community	

Part 1: Core Awareness: Prepare for the Partnership

Value	Rating	Value	Rating
Compassion		Education	
Friendship		Freedom	
Love		Family	
Loyalty		Justice	
Respect		Service	
Trust		Teamwork	
Integrity		Spirituality	
Open-mindedness			
Wealth			
Economic Stability			
Security			

What are your top four values?

Provide examples of how these values drive your professional and personal life. Be specific and detailed.

Example: Value = Family . . . My family and I sit and have dinner together every night. I call my parents/brother/sister/cousin every Sunday. We vacation with our extended family each year at a national park.

1. ....

....

....

....

....

2. ....

....

....

3. ....

4. ....

Which value(s) resonated with you the most?

Explore why these values are significant to you and how they align with your current goals and aspirations.

Do your values align with your current goals?

Evaluate the alignment between your identified values and your current goals. What discrepancies appear? How can you integrate your values more intentionally into your short-term and long-term objectives?

....

....

....

How can you prioritize conflicting values?

What values conflict? Example: Education and family could be in conflict if you want to go back to school, but worry about the impact on your family. If the assessment reveals conflicting values, how can you prioritize or reconcile these conflicts? Consider how you can navigate situations where different values may come into play.

....

....

....

In what ways can you align your personal and professional life with your values?

How you can integrate your values into both your personal and professional life? Determine specific actions or adjustments that can help you create a more values-aligned and fulfilling life.

....

....

....

What changes can you make to better live in alignment with your values?

Identify specific changes or adjustments you can make in your daily life, habits, or decision-making processes to better live in alignment with your values.

....
....
....
....

Identify your revelations so that you can explore them with your mentor after this discovery section.

....
....
....
....

Reality Reveal

....
....
....
....
....
....

Part 1: Core Awareness: Prepare for the Partnership

》》 Activity 3: Personal Vision

When you consider a mentor, it is critical to be clear about what you want so that they can help. Mentee-mentor programs require clarity to maximize your experience. When you think about your personal vision, sometimes it is a bit intimidating, but self-reflection, the awareness of where you want to go, is critical to the success of the program.

Your personal vision statement is your declaration of your aspirations, values, and goals. It is an aspirational, forward-looking statement that outlines what you hope to achieve and how best to spend your and your mentor's energy for the ultimate experience.

So, what does this look like for you? Take some time go to a quiet place and really think through this section. Be honest as you ask yourself the questions that are a part of this activity. These questions will guide you in developing your own personal vision statement.

Key elements of your personal vision may include:

Values: Your vision should align with the values that you have determined are core to you. Write them here.

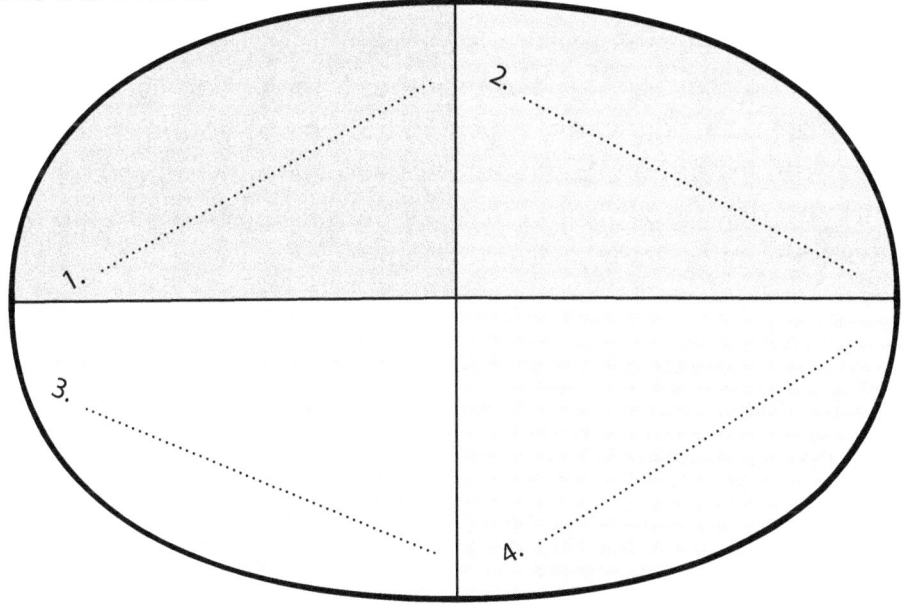

Aspirations: What influence do you aspire to have? What are your professional goals? When would you like to achieve them? What barriers are between you and those goals?

....
....
....
....
....

Inspiration and Motivation: How do you want to inspire others in the organization? When you review your vision, does it inspire, motivate, and provides the guide for your future? Why do you want to do this? What is your driving force?

....
....
....
....
....

When you create your personal vision statement, it should clarify what you really want and how your discovery work ties together with your goals. This clarity guides you to your purpose and direction, which, in turn, helps you formulate clear goals and make decisions in harmony with your aspirations. Your vision statement is based on your wants and desires and should be revisited and refined as you progress. As you evolve so does your personal vision statement.

Your personal vision statement may include aspirations for your ultimate position that align with what excites and drives you.

What position do you ultimately want to obtain?

....
....

Part 1: Core Awareness: Prepare for the Partnership

....
....
....

What do you think it takes to obtain that ultimate position?

What gives you the greatest energy and excitement as you think about your future?

What do you really want to do versus what you think you should do?

Below, draw what gives you the greatest energy and excitement.

To provide clarity to your mentor and yourself, write your vision statement using the template or blank spaces below and include components from this section. Keep in mind that you are continually evolving and that your vision will change over time.

I envision a life where my values of .... and my aspirations of ....

allow me to .... so that I ....

As you review your personal vision statement, what core elements are revealed?

Explore the fundamental aspects that shape your vision for the future, and describe how they align with your values and aspirations.

How realistic and attainable is your personal vision?

Evaluate the realism and attainability of your personal vision. Does it need to be broken down into smaller chunks to be attainable? What would that look like? What would have to happen?

You will share your thoughts with your mentor and seek their perspective on whether your vision is realistic, and if not, discuss potential adjustments to make it more achievable.

What short-term and long-term goals support your vision?

Identify specific goals, both short-term and long-term, that align with your personal vision. Prepare to discuss these goals with your mentor and explore strategies to work towards them, ensuring they contribute to the realization of your broader vision.

What obstacles or challenges might you encounter?

Anticipate potential obstacles or challenges that could hinder the realization of your personal vision. What are these and what strategies are available to overcome or avoid these challenges?

How can you continuously align your actions with your personal vision?

What strategies come to mind to maintain alignment between your daily actions and your personal vision? Explore ways to stay focused, motivated, and resilient in the face of challenges, ensuring that your actions contribute positively to your overall vision for the future.

Identify the key revelations so that you can explore them with your mentor after this discovery section. Once you have your mentor, share your thoughts, and seek their perspective on whether your vision is realistic, and if not, discuss potential adjustments or steps to make it more achievable.

Inspire To Aspire

Reality Reveal

Part 1: Core Awareness: Prepare for the Partnership

》》 Discovery Recap

You have discovered where you would like help, dove deep into your values, and created your own personal vision statement. To prepare for that all important mentor search, it's time to do a quick recap and prepare to meet your potential mentor:

What patterns or themes emerge from your discovery?

Reflect on the recurring patterns or themes identified during your discovery. Prepare to discuss these with your mentor to gain insights into your strengths, areas for improvement, and potential areas of interest.

_____

_____

_____

_____

_____

How do your values align with your aspirations?

Explore the alignment between your core values and your aspirations and vision. Prepare to discuss any discrepancies with your mentor and consider how you can integrate your values more fully into your personal and professional life.

_____

_____

_____

_____

What surprised you about the discovery?

Prepare to share any surprises, revelations, or unexpected findings from your discovery with your mentor. Discuss why these aspects were surprising and how they might influence your future goals or decisions.

....

....

....

....

....

....

....

In what areas do you seek further clarification or exploration?

Identify any areas of ambiguity or uncertainty that arose during your discovery. Prepare to discuss these with your mentor and explore strategies for gaining further clarity or conducting additional exploration to better understand yourself.

....

....

....

....

....

....

....

Part 1: Core Awareness: Prepare for the Partnership

What are your known strengths and weaknesses? How can you leverage your strengths and mitigate your weaknesses?

Identify your strengths and weaknesses. Prepare to discuss specific actions and strategies to leverage your strengths in your personal and professional life. Similarly, explore ways to mitigate or address any identified weaknesses. Your mentor can provide valuable guidance on how to maximize your strengths and minimize your weaknesses.

Reality Reveal

》》 Activity 4: Find Your Mentor

Your mentor will serve as a beacon, guiding you through the intricate paths of personal and professional growth. Your mentor will offer guidance based on experiences they have had in their careers. Your mentor should be a leader in their field imparts not only practical knowledge but also instills the qualities of visionary and thought leadership. They are to inspire you to cultivate your unique leadership style and foster the emergence of a future aspiring leader. The mentee/mentor relationship is a partnership based on trust, aligned values, commitment, and mutual respect.

QUALITIES OF A MENTOR

Experience and Expertise: A good mentor has a wealth of knowledge and experience in the field or area you are interested in.

Effective Communication: A mentor should be an excellent communicator, capable of explaining complex concepts, providing constructive feedback, and actively listening to your concerns.

Empathy and Patience: Mentors should be understanding and patient, recognizing your challenges and helping you navigate them *without judgment*.

Availability: A mentor should be accessible and willing to dedicate time to your growth. This is a time commitment for you both and each of you will have to be available for this to work.

Encouragement and Support: A good mentor should motivate and inspire you. They should believe in your potential and encourage you to strive for your goals.

Goal-Oriented: A mentor should help you set clear goals and provide guidance on how to achieve them. Your mentor should challenge you if you are missing your goals to understand the deeper why.

Networking Skills: Mentors can help you connect with other professionals in your field, expanding your network and opportunities. Who do they know? How can this help you learn more about them and you?

Part 1: Core Awareness: Prepare for the Partnership

Honesty and Constructive Feedback: A mentor should be candid in their feedback, pointing out your strengths and areas for improvement while offering suggestions for growth. *You are not looking for a cheerleader or a critic.*

Remember that mentorship is a two-way relationship. The ultimate mentor for you is someone that you can trust and is supportive but also challenges you.

Your organization may have a process to match you with a mentor. Be choosy as this is one of the most important relationships of your career. If your organization does not have a formalized mentor program, you will need to reach out directly and ask to speak with your target mentor. Write a descriptive email asking for 15 minutes of their time.

See below email example:

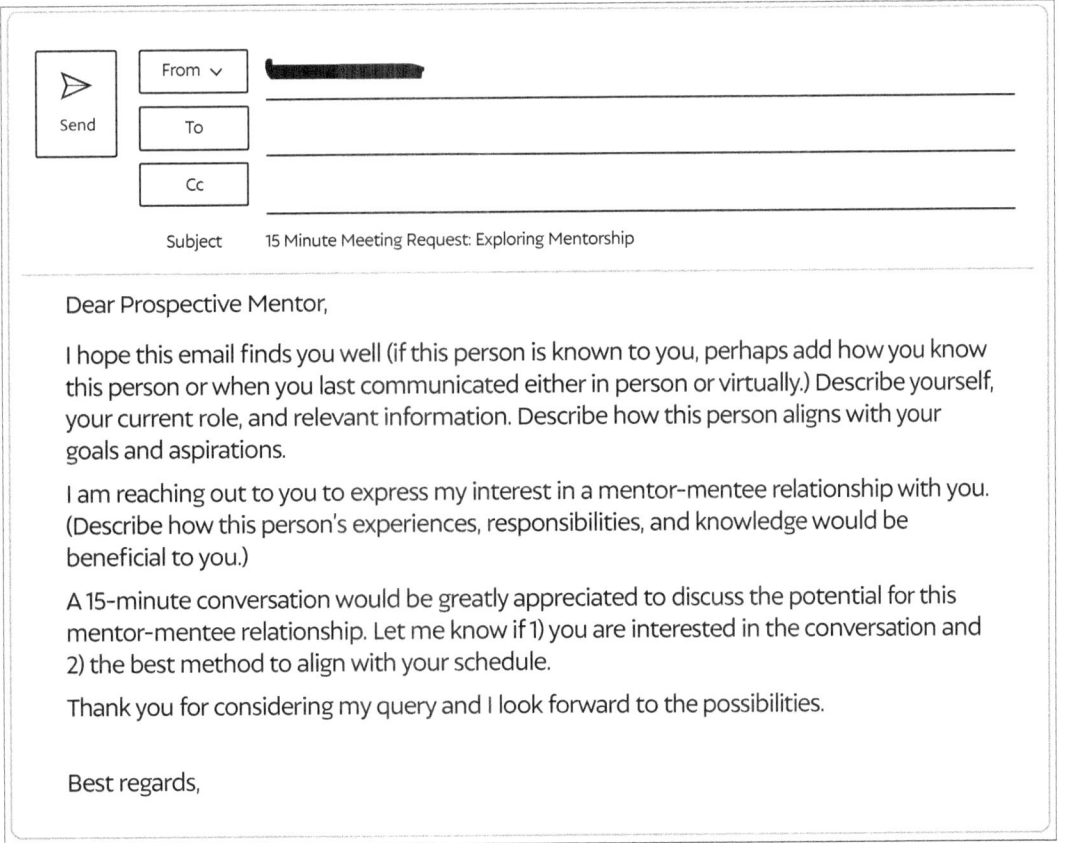

Then use the below assessment to determine the best mentor fit for you.

Imagine your ultimate mentor. What characteristics does this person have? Describe in detail the mentor that would inspire you. Who are potential mentor candidates?

....

....

....

....

....

Now that you have determined the characteristics you want and potential candidates, reach out. People are honored to be sought out as a mentor. They will appreciate that you have performed self-discovery and have a general idea of what inspires you, what you aspire to be, and how they can help you. Who do you know that might align with these characteristics?

....

....

....

....

....

The mentorship is a two-way street and you should contribute. These contributions could be related to what you see within your affiliations or experiences. Perhaps it is with technologies or exposure to other types of communications and networks not known to your mentor. What do you expect to contribute to the mentoring process?

....

....

....

....

....

Part 1: Core Awareness: Prepare for the Partnership

Following are questions to ask your potential future mentor: This section is intended to help you understand if this person could be your mentor before you launch the official mentorship process outlined below, chemistry meeting.

Use these questions to evaluate your potential mentor before you begin a journey with your mentor to ensure time optimization for the ultimate experience. You may use these as "interview" questions or calibration questions before launching into the partnership. This provides a framework to see if this mentor can truly inspire you to your aspirations.

What professional experience and expertise do you think would be valuable to a mentee, like me? What stories can you share with me about pivotal moments in your professional career?

Understanding your mentor's background and expertise is crucial. Ask about their professional experience, skills, and knowledge to ensure that their strengths align with your goals and areas of interest.

_____

_____

_____

_____

_____

What type of mentoring style do you prefer?

Discussing mentoring styles is essential for a successful mentor-mentee relationship. Ask your potential mentor about their preferred mentoring approach, whether it is more hands-on where you work on homework topics during the session, advisory where you provide examples or challenges you face and ask for advice, or a combination, and determine if it aligns with your learning preferences. Your mentor may prefer to receive an email outlining topics to discuss, concerns and questions you may have so that your mentor can prepare for the meeting with you.

_____

_____

How much time can you commit to mentoring?

Clarify the time commitment your mentor can offer. Discuss the frequency and duration of meetings or interactions to ensure that it aligns with your expectations and needs for guidance and support. This program is designed for sessions every other week for several months.

Have you mentored others with similar goals or backgrounds?

Inquire about your mentor's past mentoring experiences, especially those with mentees who share similar goals, challenges, or backgrounds as yours. This can provide insights into their ability to guide and support someone with your specific needs.

Part 1: Core Awareness: Prepare for the Partnership

What are your expectations for our mentoring partnership?

You will discuss expectations during the chemistry meeting. What questions come to mind? How do they see your role in the mentoring relationship, as well as their expectations of what they can provide? This will help establish clear boundaries and ensure a mutually beneficial partnership.

....

....

....

....

Share your vision and brief areas of interest with your mentor based on the discovery recap. Are these areas that the mentor is comfortable with?

....

....

....

....

Reality Reveal

....

....

....

....

....

....

⟫ Activity 5: Chemistry Meeting

So, you have reflected on what you are looking for, found your mentor and it is your first meeting. How do you start?

Get to know each other. If you have not already, look them up on LinkedIn. What interests do they have, organizations they are associated with and what is their career path? Think of three questions that you are curious about.

....
....
....
....
....

Share a bit about yourself and why they were chosen by you.

....
....
....
....
....
....

RULES OF ENGAGEMENT:

Establish Rules of Engagement: This very important step is sometimes missed. Below you can find rules of engagement suggestions with alignment questions to ensure mutual understanding. Agree on the definition of words such as confidentiality, honesty, and off limits? This creates alignment and trust in the relationship. Space is provided for rules of engagement not listed.

Frequency of Meetings and Commitment: How often should we meet? We recommend every two weeks. What happens if something interferes? What is our agreement to notify each other? How can we keep our commitments?

Time commitment: Define your time commitment. What will be our agreement during and after this partnership? How long should this take?

_____
_____
_____
_____

Communication Avenues: What is the best method to communicate? Chat, email, phone? Under what circumstance(s)?

_____
_____
_____
_____

Homework: The mentee is expected to do work between meetings. Assignments are laid out in this playbook to guide you. What is the commitment to getting and doing the homework? What happens if it is not complete? What if there are questions between sessions? There are blank pages for the mentee to track the sessions. How will these be utilized?

_____
_____
_____
_____

Confidentiality: Define confidentiality. What is our confidentiality agreement during and after this partnership?

....

....

....

....

....

Honesty: Define honesty. What do we agree that honesty will mean in this relationship?

....

....

....

....

....

Off Limits: What are off limits, such as personal information? How do we tell the other person that something is off limits? These could also be defined as emotional triggers.

....

....

....

....

....

Part 1: Core Awareness: Prepare for the Partnership

(blank for you to add another ground rule)

_____
_____
_____
_____
_____
_____
_____

(blank for you to add another ground rule)

_____
_____
_____
_____
_____
_____
_____

Closure of Mentorship: How will we close this out? What are our ideas?

_____
_____
_____
_____
_____
_____
_____

EXPECTATIONS:

Create expectations from each party on goals, length, and success factors of mentorship.

Review your responses prior to the first meeting.

What are your expectations of this mentorship?

_____
_____
_____
_____

How long will this take? Perhaps review the proposed timeline located in the back of the playbook and handbook as a reference. Is this reasonable? Doable? Fair?

_____
_____
_____
_____

At the end of this partnership, how would you measure success? This may be a good opportunity to review the midterm and final calibration tools.

_____
_____
_____
_____

Additional Mentor Questions for Your Consideration

What specific goals or outcomes do you envision for our mentor/mentee partnership?

Encourage the mentor to articulate the specific goals or outcomes they hope to achieve through the mentor/mentee partnership. This question helps set clear expectations and provides a roadmap for you to understand the purpose of the mentorship experience.

How can you best support my professional growth and development?

Ask your mentor about their expectations of your role in supporting your growth and development. Understanding how you can contribute to your goals provides clarity of your needs and objectives for the relationship.

What key areas or skills do you hope to share or enhance through this relationship?

Inquire about the mentor's focus areas and the skills or knowledge they aim to share or enhance with the mentee. This question helps define the mentor's purpose in the relationship and provides the mentee with a clear understanding of what they can gain from the mentorship.

....

....

....

....

Reality Reveal

....

....

....

....

....

....

> "IF YOU THINK YOU CAN OR YOU THINK YOU CAN'T, YOU ARE RIGHT."
> —HENRY FORD

Part 2

Core Behaviors: Personal View

Activity 1: Work and Home Friction
Activity 2: Emotional Intelligence
Activity 3: Getting out of Your Own Head
Activity 4: Goal Setting
Activity 5: Career Transition
Activity 6: Visibility and Influence
Activity 7: Confidence
Activity 8: Risk and Initiative
Mid-term Calibration
Reflect and What's Next

》》 Activity 1: Work and Home Friction

We have been told about the need for balance between work and home. *Spoiler alert: There is no such thing as balance. You are only one person. You are not a home person and a separate work person. Everything is competing for your time and energy and supply is limited.*

What people experience is the friction between home and work. In both realms of life, there are sacrifices that are made as we prioritize conflicts and navigate the friction. With the added complexity of work from home and hybrid work, this can be even more of a challenge. Understanding your boundaries is the key to creating a balance between work and home.

Work

Whether you work at your employer's location, your home office, or anywhere else, consider these next few questions:

How do you designate your workspace? Do you have a separate room? Is it a cubicle, office, shared space? Is your workspace the kitchen table?

....

....

....

How do you communicate your "do not disturb" in your environment? This could be a sign on the door, a door closed or something that communicates "do not disturb."

....

....

....

How do you get "ready for work"? Some people that work from home, will shower, change into work clothes, and treat their home office as if it was their office or not.

What rules have you established such as office hours, break time, do not disturb time? What are your typical work hours? Is it the same when you work from home or from the office? How do you use notifications? Are you always "available"?

Home

Most of us take our work home with us. We are connected through our devices. It is a fact. With the "always on" environment, you must be very deliberate with your boundaries to manage the flexibility and corresponding anxiety.

When you work from home, how do you separate home from work?

How can you focus on just home when you are home? Where is your computer or work phone? How often do you check your devices? What is the expectation from your manager?

What ground rules have you established for yourself when it comes to working at home? Who have you communicated this to? What would they say if you gave them your work from home rules?

How are you taking care of yourself? Sleep, eating, and exercise? How many hours do you sleep at night? Are you rested when you awaken? What is your eating schedule? Do you miss meals? How often? How much exercise do you do each week?

"**Stop**, **Start**, **Continue**" is a great tool to create the space to truly separate work and home and reduce the friction. As you think about the above questions, what should you stop, what should you start, what should you continue? Utilizing the various topics create a plan to reduce the friction using the below format.

Stop: To create appropriate boundaries and reduce friction between home and work, what will you stop doing? When will you stop?

....
....
....
....
....

Start: To create appropriate boundaries and reduce friction between home and work, what will you start doing? When will you start?

....
....
....
....
....

Continue: To maintain appropriate boundaries and maintain healthy friction between home and work, what will you continue?

....
....
....
....
....

As you think about the things that you plan to stop, start, or continue, commit to yourself that you will make these a priority. Select one from each category and finish the below sentence. Each day remind yourself what you are committed to doing. What is measured is actioned. Share this with an accountability partner to keep you accountable. What part of the above start, stop continue will be most difficult to do? Who can help you be successful with your plan?

....

....

....

....

....

To track progress, use the below tool:

At the end of each day, rate yourself using a scale of 1 to 10. This tool is an inspiration from Marshall Goldsmith's tool in Triggers.

     1 = I did not do very well today.

     10 = I did a great job today.

Track this for a week or two as what is measured is actioned. What did you discover?

Start: Did I do my best to . . .

....

....

....

....

....

Part 2: Core Behaviors: Personal View

Stop: Did I do my best to. . .

Continue: Did I do my best to. . .

Question for Mentor: How do you manage home and work? What works well and what have you tried that just does not work?

Reality Reveal

>>> Activity 2: Emotional Intelligence

The term "Emotional Intelligence" first appeared in 1964. However, it gained popularity in the 1995 best-selling book *Emotional Intelligence*, by Daniel Goleman.

If someone has High Emotional Intelligence, they possess skills that enable them to recognize, manage, and effectively use both their own emotions and those of others. Emotional intelligence is multifaceted and can include key components such as emotion **recognition**, **understanding**, and **management**, as well as **empathy**, **social skills**, **self-awareness**, and **motivation**.

Self-assess yourself on your skills in this area. Circle which one is the most reflective most of the time.

Emotional recognition means that you can accurately identify your emotions and the emotions of others. You identify these emotions by using verbal and nonverbal cues. How do you know if you are upset or if others are upset?

I've got this   Needs improvement   Help Needed

Emotional understanding means that you understand the causes and consequences of various emotions in both yourself and others. How well do you react to your emotions or those of others?

I've got this   Needs improvement   Help Needed

Emotion management is self-regulation of emotions. You can adapt to anger, stress, or other strong emotions without becoming overwhelmed and reactionary. How calm are you in stressful situations?

I've got this   Needs improvement   Help Needed

Empathy is the ability to sense and share feelings of others. There is genuine concern for the well-being of others and is skilled in listening, offering support and not judging. Can you meet the other person where they are instead of where you think they should be?

I've got this   Needs improvement   Help Needed

Part 2: Core Behaviors: Personal View

Social skills are the ability to communicate effectively, resolve conflict, and build positive relationships. They can navigate social situations with ease. How successful are you with conflict resolution and building positive relationships?

I've got this   Needs improvement   Help Needed

Self-awareness is just how it sounds. To be aware of how emotions affect you and how to deal with them. They have a clear and accurate perception of strengths and weaknesses. Can you identify your strengths and weaknesses and how it affects those around you?

I've got this   Needs improvement   Help Needed

Motivation can be intrinsic or extrinsic. Intrinsic motivation is the ability to harness your emotions and focus on the task at hand even at the face of challenges. How easy is it for you to bounce back from setbacks or failures?

I've got this   Needs improvement   Help Needed

When you look at these facets of emotional intelligence, which ones need improvement and where do you really need the help? How can you maximize those that you do well and create a plan around those that need help?

Question for Mentor: Where and when do you most struggle with these facets of emotional intelligence? What tools do you use or how do you manage through these?

Reality Reveal

....
....
....
....
....
....

》》 Activity 3: Getting Out of Your Own Head

So many of us are just stuck in our own heads. Even if you try to tell yourself *mind over matter*, sometimes it is not enough. The best way to get out of your own head is to figure out what is holding you back. Fear is the leading reason that folks cannot get out of their own head. Other reasons can be limiting beliefs or what could be perceived as impostor syndrome.

WHAT ARE YOU AFRAID OF?

Fear comes in many forms. Fear of looking stupid, fear of not having the answer, fear of the unknown, or fear that you are just not good enough.

So, when you cannot get out of your own head, consider what it is that you are afraid of. Be as detailed in your answer as possible. Is it getting up in front of a room full of people? Is it presenting information that you are not sure will be accepted? Is it leading a new team or project, or something you have never done before?

What are you afraid of? Take a few minutes to write down your fears that stop you from achieving your aspirations. These may be fear of looking stupid, fear of getting it wrong, fear of failure, etc.

How and when do these fears reveal themselves? Be very specific and use who, what, when, and where.

How do these fears stop you from fulfilling your aspirations?

What techniques have you tried to combat these fears that worked well or did not work?

LIMITING BELIEFS:

Limiting beliefs are those beliefs that you are just not good enough. This may be from the words spoken to you, to others or about others. This may be from behaviors you have witnessed or subjected to good or bad. This may be due to your comparison to others. These limiting beliefs can be debilitating. It can stop you from reaching your ultimate goals.

Take time to write below a list of limiting beliefs. Next, rewrite these as aspirational beliefs.

Examples:
- I am not a good presenter.–I can be a good presenter if I practice.
- I do not know all the details of the subject.–I know enough about the subject and how to find the answers to the part that I do not know.

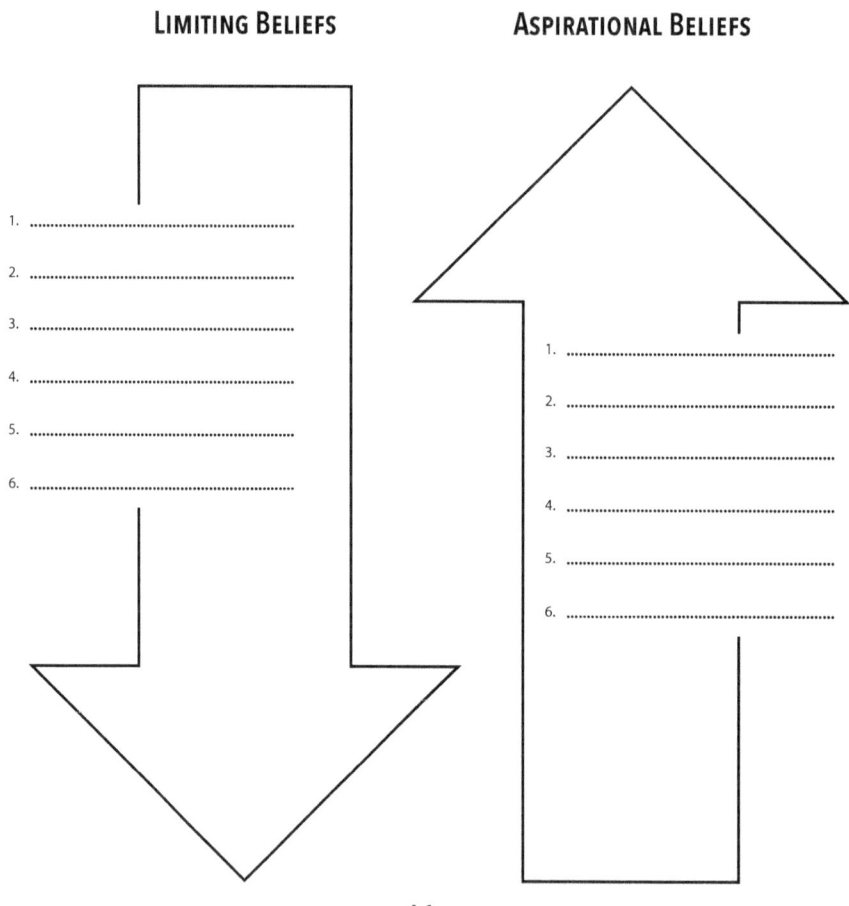

What would your world look like if you replaced the limiting belief with your aspirational belief? What would have to happen?

....
....
....
....
....
....

Next time the limiting belief comes to mind, where are you, what is happening, who are you with? Then practice with your aspirational belief. What challenges you to this new aspirational belief? How can you conquer this limiting belief?

....
....
....
....
....

IMPOSTOR SYNDROME:

Impostor syndrome refers to a psychological phenomenon in which individuals, despite external evidence of their competence, skills, or accomplishments, consistently doubt their own abilities and fear being exposed as frauds. People experiencing what can be perceived as impostor syndrome often believe that their success is a result of luck or other external factors, rather than their own capabilities. They have an internalized fear of being "found out" as an impostor in their field or profession.

Impostor syndrome was first coined by psychologists Pauline R. Clance and Suzanne A. Imes.

To determine whether you may experience symptoms or what could be perceived as impostor syndrome, consider the following:

Do you often feel like your achievements are due to luck or external factors rather than your own abilities?

Do you have difficulty internalizing your successes and feel that they are not a true reflection of your competence?

Do you frequently worry that others will discover you are not as capable as they think you are?

Do you set exceptionally high standards for yourself and fear you will fall short, even when you meet or exceed these standards?

Do you downplay your accomplishments or attribute them to factors other than your own skills and hard work?

If you answer "yes" to these questions, describe the circumstance. Be specific with who, what, when, and where as this may provide clues to situations where this is most prominent.

_____

_____

_____

_____

What would it take for you to recognize yourself and your accomplishments?

_____

_____

_____

_____

Part 2: Core Behaviors: Personal View

Question for Mentor: When have you, or someone known to you, suffered fear, limiting beliefs or impostor syndrome? What did you do?

Reality Reveal

»» Activity 4: Goal Setting

Reflect on your ability to set and achieve your goals. Perhaps you are good at setting goals, but they are not achievable. Many times, our intent is not to fail to achieve our goals, but something gets in the way. As you set goals, are they fair, doable? What help or collaboration is needed for success? *Tip: Goals that align with your values and passions tend to be more successful.*

When did you set a goal and it failed? Describe the goal below.

....
....
....
....

Now let us look at this goal with fresh eyes. Was it a **S.M.A.R.T.** (Specific, Measurable, Achievable, Relevant, Time-bound) goal? How was it defined by these criteria? How would you revise the failed goal to be S.M.A.R.T.? Describe below:

SPECIFIC

....
....
....
....
....

MEASURABLE

....
....

Part 2: Core Behaviors: Personal View

Achievable

Relevant

Time-bound

Describe the benefits of setting a goal using the **S.M.A.R.T.** format.

How can you boost your motivation when you work toward a goal?

What are the obstacles to setting and achieving your goals?

Create a **S.M.A.R.T.** goal for something that you want to accomplish short-term.

Question for Mentor: What process do you use to create and maintain goals?

Reality Reveal

》》 Activity 5: Career Transition

No matter where you are in your career, a transition either has happened or will happen. These transitions could be a promotion, industry shift, economic factors, changes in education, or geographic changes.

What stage are you in – considering, transitioning, or transitioned? Successful career transitions involve planning, learning, and seeking support.

Describe where you are in your career transition or describe a past transition.

....
....
....
....
....

CONSIDERING:

If you are considering a career transition, create your dream job description with as much detail as possible including anticipated position requirements.

....
....
....
....
....
....
....

Part 2: Core Behaviors: Personal View

Now, reflect on what your proposed job description. What is missing? How does this compare with your current role?

What roles within your organization align with this job description? What experience, skills or knowledge deficiencies do you have, if any?

What should be your next steps? How can you obtain the understanding of the expectations for the role?

If there is not a role that aligns with your aspirations, where can you investigate? How can your mentor help you?

....

....

....

....

TRANSITIONING:

Transitioning from one role to another within the same organization, or a new organization, requires patience, humility, and a willingness to learn. You can start this process by meeting with your team, peers, customers (both internal and external), and your manager.

Using the three simple questions: what you know, what you do not know, and what you think you know about the role and expectations of the role, you can prepare to have one on ones with your new team.

Practice using the above three simple questions. What did this reveal? Was it similar among your teammates?

....

....

....

....

What responses surprised you?

....

....

....

Part 2: Core Behaviors: Personal View

_____

_____

How can you take this information and use it to guide your communications with the team?

_____

_____

_____

_____

Three other questions to ask the stakeholders such as internal customers, external customers, peers, and leadership could be:

What is your expectation of this role?

_____

_____

_____

_____

What are some complexities that I should understand that may not be relatively apparent?

_____

_____

_____

_____

What is your preferred form of communication?

....
....
....
....
....
....

How can I best help you be successful?

....
....
....
....
....
....

What priorities do you envision for the next 90 days?

....
....
....
....
....
....

TRANSITIONED:

You have already transitioned into a new role and things could be better.

Have you shared your vision statement with the stakeholders? Where do they fit into this vision statement? Use the three questions of what we should stop, start, and continue to create a dialogue with the team.

Write below your vision and challenges you see.

_____
_____
_____
_____
_____
_____

How you would communicate your vision and the challenges with your new team?

_____
_____
_____
_____

Use a stop, start continue technique to see what are the issues that need attention. Then using the "what is possible?" question, from their feedback, what steps are doable and possible so that you can create a feedback loop to your team. Not everything will be possible, that is OK and should be communicated as to what it is and why that is a challenge or not possible at this time. This creates a team where they feel heard.

What did the team think should be stopped? What is possible?

What did the team think should be started? What is possible?

What did the team think should be continued? What is possible?

What surprised you about these responses?

Part 2: Core Behaviors: Personal View

How can you take this information and use it to guide your communications and changes within the team?

How will you communicate in a way to show that they were heard?

Question for Mentor: When did you experience a great and a not-so-great career transition? What did you learn?

Reality Reveal

⫸ Activity 6: Visibility and Influence

Visibility is the level of recognition, awareness, and prominence an individual has within an organization. Visibility is an essential part of professional success, career advancement, and effective teamwork. Visibility can be achieved by delivering high quality results, effective communication both upwards and downwards, contribution on important projects, and networking. Visibility can be defined as creating a positive impact, that benefits not only the individual, but also the team and the organization.

VISIBILITY:

How do you want the organization to see you?

Do you want the organization to see you as a team player, a go getter, a knowledgeable leader, a high potential, someone who cares, a risk taker, or what?

....
....
....
....

What does that look like today?

Describe how you believe you are viewed today. Be specific as it could be different in different circumstances and even with different people.

....
....
....
....
....

Part 2: Core Behaviors: Personal View

What gaps appear from how you want the organization to see you and how you believe they see you today?

....
....
....
....
....
....

What steps can you take to close that gap? What is stopping you?

....
....
....
....
....
....

How can your mentor help you gain the visibility you are looking for?

....
....
....
....
....
....

INFLUENCE:

Influence is the ability for the individual to affect the thoughts, decisions, actions, and opinions of others. Influence can drive positive change, gain support, and shape the direction of the company. Your ability to influence is based on your credibility, ability to communicate persuasively, relationships, problem-solving, and teamwork. *Tip: Curiously watch others and how they influence others.*

Refer to the question you asked yourself when creating your vision statement. How do you want to inspire others in the organization? After the weeks of self-assessments and mentorship, what does that question look like now? Write it below.

How do you want to inspire others in the organization?

_____
_____
_____
_____
_____
_____

Are you at the influence level that you aspire to be? What would that look like? Describe an influential person that inspires you.

_____
_____
_____
_____
_____
_____

Part 2: Core Behaviors: Personal View

How do they appear as it pertains to credibility, ability to communicate persuasively, relationships, problem-solving, and teamwork?

_____
_____
_____
_____
_____
_____
_____
_____

Rate yourself on the influence aspects below. This would be a great opportunity to request feedback from someone else. Compare their ratings with your own ratings.

What are your next steps to gain feedback on the below influence aspirations?

_____
_____
_____
_____
_____
_____
_____
_____

Reflect on your past projects and experiences.

1. How **credible** are you? Credible in this context means being believable, trustworthy, and reliable in both actions and words.

2. Rate your ability to **communicate persuasively**. This means your ability not just to discuss the topic but persuade in a way that shows your understanding of the topic, the logic, and the ability to move someone to action.

3. Rate yourself on your **relationships** with other numbers of the team, peers, and leadership.

4. How good are you at **problem-solving**?

5. When you think about **teamwork** where would you rate yourself and your ability to build consensus, listen to others, and work toward a common goal.

Summarize your assessment in the table provided and rate yourself from 1 to 5 where 5 means "I got this!" Ask a friend or colleague for a similar assessment using the above questions and document in table below.

Part 2: Core Behaviors: Personal View

Aspect	Your Assessment	External Assessment	Gap
Credibility			
Persuasiveness			
Relationships			
Problem Solving			
Teamwork			

What insights did you gain from this experience?

What are the largest gaps? What do you think is missing?

What steps can you take to close these gaps?

How would you use your influence to help yourself, others, and the organization?

....
....
....
....
....

Question for Mentor: What input do you have on my self-ratings? What do you think the one thing I could do to impact my visibility and influence?

Reality Reveal

....
....
....
....
....
....

⫸ Activity 7: Confidence

A confident leader is one that is an effective communicator, is open to feedback, decisive, resilient, empowers others, and has a strong vision. A non-confident leader may appear insecure, overconfident, be inflexible, defensive, and micromanaging. Some confident leaders have insecurities that are masked by bravado vs. confidence. For someone who inspires to be more confident, has trouble making decisions, or having conversations with others, the following exercises could be helpful.

IMAGINE FUTURE

Imagination is a great thing. It bypasses reality so that you can imagine a future that does not yet exist. Envisioning your future allows you to experience the situation now. Think about a time either in the past, present, or in the future that you are uncertain about.

ANTICIPATE THE SITUATION

What is the topic, what are you wearing, who is your audience, where are you? Begin to create a picture of what this looks like. Write it out as if it were today at this moment.

_____

_____

_____

_____

_____

_____

_____

What challenges do you envision? How would these challenges be addressed?

....
....
....
....
....
....
....

What are the questions that might be asked by members of the audience? *Tip: Imagine you were a member of the audience, what would you ask?*

....
....
....
....
....
....
....

Have you socialized your idea? If so, with whom. What feedback was provided?

....
....
....
....
....
....
....

PRACTICE YOUR PITCH

There is nothing better than practicing. Watch *Ted Talks*. Look how smooth and deliberate these speakers appear, with excellent timing techniques. Why? Because they practice, practice, practice before they pitch.

Find someone you trust and pitch to them. Have them pretend to be a member that you are presenting to.

Describe the situation and who would you practice with?

_____

_____

_____

_____

_____

What questions would they ask you?

_____

_____

_____

_____

How can you better prepare?

_____

_____

_____

_____

What did you learn by this exercise?

....
....
....
....
....

Maybe practice with a member that you think will be a challenge. *Tip: Pick someone who is not yet aligned with your idea. It will surprise them, and you will gain insights and influence.*

What feedback did they give you? What surprised you?

....
....
....
....
....

What did you learn by this exercise?

....
....
....
....
....
....

What changes will you make to your pitch?

Script for Success

Having a "Script for Success" allows you to write down what you will say and walk through the meeting ahead of time. It will help you prepare your answers for the questions that might come up. You can even have a meeting before the meeting to ensure all parties are on board, know their role, and help anticipate any challenges.

Situational use example: You have an opportunity to negotiate a big contract with a client. Your boss will not be attending, but she is expecting a great outcome that is beneficial to the company in a big way. You know some of the members from your team will be in the meeting to support and provide answers as needed. You know some of the client's attendees.

The best and most effective way to achieve success is to script it.

Describe in detail what you think the big wins are that you will need to ensure. What are the areas that you can give up? What are the most important aspects for you? Your client?

What members of your team are aligned or not? For successful scripting, all members must be in alignment. This does not mean agreement. What are these alignments? Is there a need to have a meeting before the meeting to ensure alignment?

What allies do you have that can provide insights into what is important to the client? What are those items? Any concerns?

What would be the best possible outcome?

After you use this method, what did you learn? How would you do this differently next time?

What are some other ways you gained confidence around something you have not done before? Remember we all put our pants on one leg at a time. We all appear much more confident than we truly are. Even those who seem to be always on point have fears.

Question for Mentor: How do you appear confident? What tricks or tools do you use?

Reality Reveal

⫸ Activity 8: Risk-taking and Initiative

Let us be clear. Those who sit on their hands do not get promoted. When was the last time you raised your hand for something no one else wanted to do? Have you looked around and wondered why you did not get that project or promotion?

Risk-taking has many benefits. Risk-taking can lead to innovation, learning and improvements. When you take risks, visibility, good or bad, will happen. *Tip: It took 40 attempts to the formula right for WD40, hence, the name.*

COMFORT ZONE VS. STRETCH ZONE

The comfort zone is a place that is familiar and safe. You are in your element, and you can perform your tasks easily. This is also a place of low risk and low challenge. Therefore, there is little room for growth and development. Although this is a place of ease and predictability, it can lead to stagnation and risks your relevancy.

Working through your stretch zone is both challenging and growth oriented. There is more risk with more opportunity and the need to be more agile is greater. The stretch zone, if constant, can lead to stress. You will have to determine your appropriate mix of comfort zone and stretch zone. However, when you stretch, it presents an opportunity for development and growth.

What does your comfort zone look like? How committed are you to stretch beyond your comfort zone?

What does your stretch zone look like? How much are you willing to stretch?

What might happen if you stay in your comfort zone?

What can you practice that is outside of your comfort zone?

When you reached outside of your comfort zone, what did you learn about yourself? What surprised you?

WHAT IS POSSIBLE?

This is a great question when everyone is against your idea. It provides a forum of possibilities that may have otherwise been ignored.

How can you use this question in a way to inspire risk-taking within an organization, team, project?

_____
_____
_____
_____
_____
_____

What are the benefits of using such a question?

_____
_____
_____
_____
_____

How do you think others will respond? What do you think is possible?

_____
_____
_____
_____
_____

Question for Mentor: How important do you believe risk taking and initiative are to my development and goals? When have you taken a risk and it went well or did not go as well as planned? What happened?

Reality Reveal

....
....
....
....
....
....

»» Mid-Term Calibration

You have completed the three to four aspects of personal behaviors and are halfway through your time with your mentor. Use this calibration tool to ensure alignment with your and your mentor's expectations.

What progress have you made and what obstacles do you face?

Review your initial expectations and vision as you embarked on this mentoring program, where are you vs. where you want to be. What remains as you launch into the second half of this journey?

_____
_____
_____
_____
_____
_____

What is working and not working as it pertains to commitments, topics, ground rules, engagement, etc.?

_____
_____
_____
_____
_____

What feedback have you received from others?

As you make changes and learn new tools, the people you work with may notice some changes. Have people noticed? Have you noticed any changes including awareness?

....
....
....
....

What part of this process do you love and what part of this process do you hate? Be honest with yourself and your mentor to gain a deeper perspective of what is working and enjoyable and what may cause stress and uncertainties.

....
....
....
....

What should you and your mentor start, stop or continue as you launch the second stage of this partnership?

....
....
....
....

Reflection and What's Next

PART ONE

Review your initial expectation found at the end of the first section. Reflect on where you were, where you are, and where you still might want to go.

Write your initial expectation below:

_____
_____
_____
_____

What part of this expectation was achieved or not achieved? If so, how will you take this further? If not, what factors got in the way?

_____
_____
_____
_____

What were the top three takeaways from your experience with your mentor?

_____
_____
_____
_____

Attach a before and after picture of yourself in the space provided below.

How will you take these three takeaways into your future?

....

....

....

....

What did you learn about being a mentee and, potentially, a future mentor?

How has this relationship shaped your future self?

How would you like to sunset this partnership? What would that look like?

Part Two

Create a 30/60/90-day plan around the personal behaviors you have worked on with your mentor. Then, create a future vision of yourself one year and five years from now. This provides guidance for future developments, conversations, and growth. Take an opportunity to discuss this with your mentor how they would like to participate in your future success.

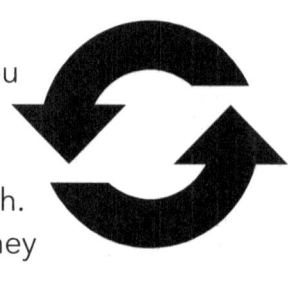

What behaviors did you prioritize? Create a plan that identifies what you will stop, start, and continue. How will that translate to your aspirations?

What behaviors would you develop further? How do you want to develop these?

....
....
....

Start:

....
....
....
....

Stop:

....
....
....
....

Continue:

How can your current mentor assist you? Is your current mentor able and willing to assist you? Who inspires you as you think about further aspirations? This is a great check in point as you launch the global topics.

Write your initial vision:

What is your new vision at this point in the mentorship program?

Look back on your vision statement and restate using a one-year marker and a five-year marker. How does that vision change? What aspects are the same?

What is your vision 1 year from today?

What is your vision 5 years from today?

Part 2: Core Behaviors: Personal View

What needs to happen for you to realize your revised vision(s)?

Question for Mentor: Share your plan and future vision with your mentor. What do you think is my biggest obstacle in aspiring to these plans and visions?

Reality Reveal

"Excellence is never an accident. It is always the result of high intention, sincere effort, and intelligent execution; it represents the wise choice of many alternatives—choice, not chance, determines your destiny."

—Aristotle

Part 3

Core Connections: Global View

Activity 1: Networking
Activity 2: Organizational Culture
Activity 3: Navigating Corporate Politics
Activity 4: Allyships
Final Calibration
Partnership Sunset

》》 Activity 1: Networking

Networking can be very intimidating. In its simplest form it is building relationships within the business community. In business, the focus of networking is to share information, obtain insights, and socialize with other like-minded individuals. Benefits could include opportunity identification, knowledge sharing, career advancement, access to resources, and brand building.

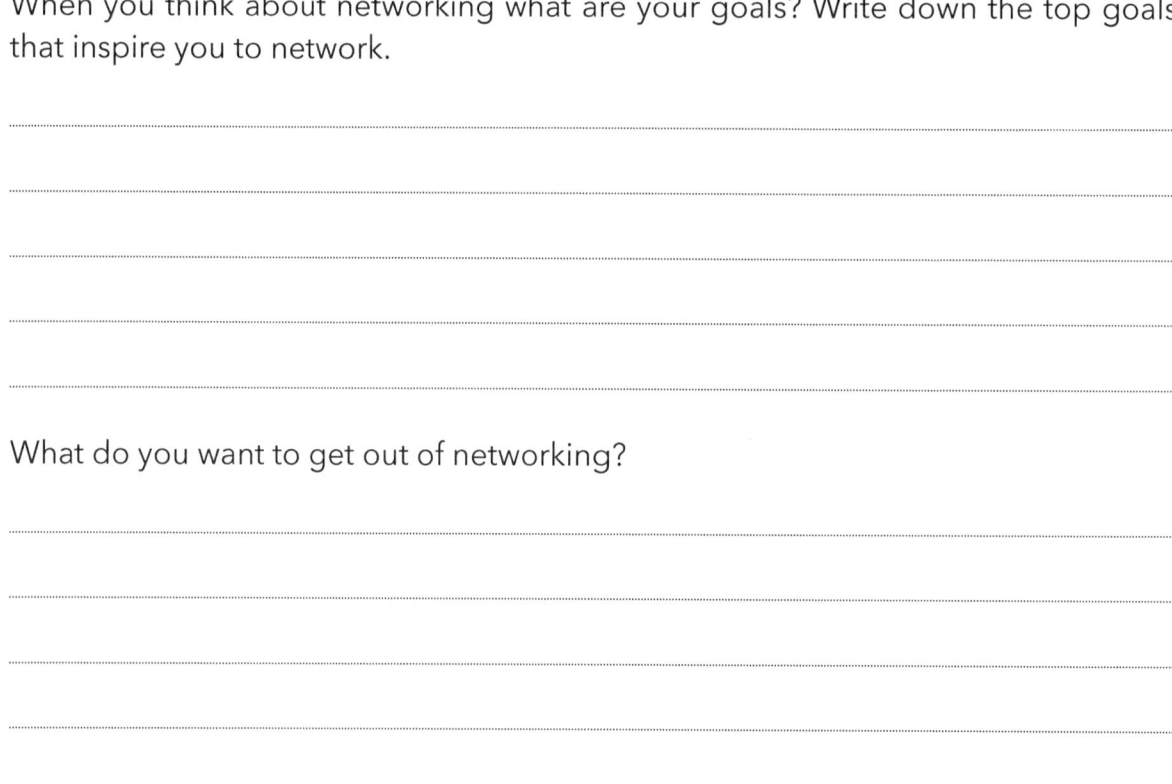

When you think about networking what are your goals? Write down the top goals that inspire you to network.

....
....
....
....
....

What do you want to get out of networking?

....
....
....
....
....

Networking can open doors to new experiences, people, opportunities, points of view, etc. How would networking help you achieve your aspirations?

Think about some of the challenges around networking. One factor may be time constraints. Networking takes time away from other interests and passions. It is important to determine what works for you, whether it is part of your existing connections such as schools, churches, team affiliations or if you should branch outside of this arena to expand your network either in person or virtually. It is important to discover your commitment to networking to determine the best use of your time. *Tip: Try a few different options. It's OK if it is not a right fit.*

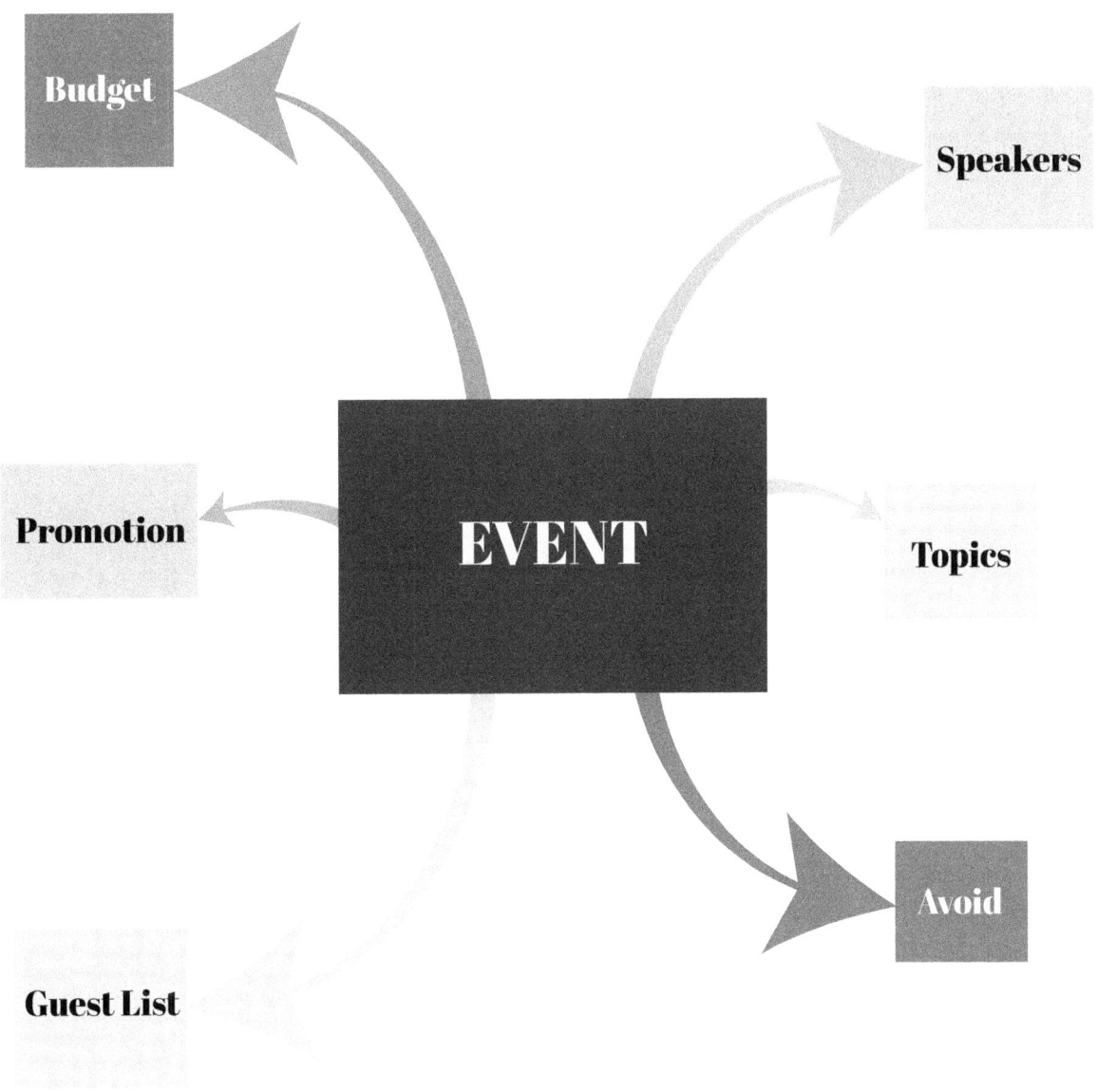

Another challenge is the fear of rejection. We all walk in a room and unless we know someone it feels like a sea of strangers. Who do we approach? How do we approach them? No one wants to come off as cheesy. Which brings us to authenticity. Everyone recalls a car salesman that pretends to like you. At the end of the day, they just wanted to sell you a car. That is not you! How do you get past that feeling or idea of inauthenticity?

_____

_____

_____

_____

How will you prepare yourself to go into a networking event when fear is stopping you? Do you go with a friend? Do you know some of the participants? What areas do you feel more comfortable? How can you align those feelings of comfort in this new arena?

_____

_____

_____

_____

When you think about networking what are your greatest fears? Identifying these fears will bring you one step closer to taming them. Write down your biggest fears and how they hold you back from achieving the goals that you set for yourself while networking.

_____

_____

_____

_____

Part 3: Core Connections: Global View

When you think about your goals for networking, what ways can you network that are true to you and help you achieve your goals? You may not have thought about this but there are many ways to network besides networking events. These may be in person events, fundraisers, corporate events, school gatherings, social parties, conferences, training sessions etc. *Tip: Practice active listening . . . Let them talk! It takes the pressure off you.*

_____
_____
_____
_____
_____
_____
_____

What events are coming up that you might have an opportunity to network? Think about what your strategy will be. Will it be to meet new people, build relationships, or ask that question that you have been wanting to ask but never had the opportunity? This is your chance.

_____
_____
_____
_____
_____
_____
_____
_____
_____

Inspire To Aspire

Create a plan for an upcoming event based on what you have learned in this activity.

Who would you like to speak with? And why? What are some questions that you really want to know the answer to?

....

....

What value do you bring to share? Each of us have unique abilities, expertise, networks, etc. How can you leverage what you know to help others?

....

....

How did it go? What will you change?

....

....

Question for Mentor: What does networking for you look like? Do you have any go to questions or intros?

Reality Reveal

....

....

....

....

....

....

》》 Activity 2: Corporate Culture

Corporate culture is the personality of the organization. It is the values, behaviors, and practices on how employees, clients, community, and other stakeholders are treated and things get done at an organization. As it pertains to the employee, it centers around how an employee sees themselves as a part of this culture and the way that they perform their work, communicate, collaborate, grow, and learn.

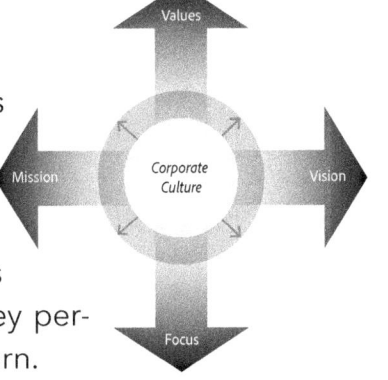

Think about your current corporation or maybe even an organization you are considering.

Define the corporate culture of your current or potential organization.

....

....

....

....

....

How does your current or potential organization's mission and vision resonate with you?

When you think about the mission and vision of either your current organization or another organization, what portions(s) of the organization's vision and/or mission inspire you?

....

....

....

....

How do the values of your organization or potential organization, align or not align with your values? How do you know? Define a corporate culture that really speaks to you.

_____
_____
_____
_____
_____

Define a corporate culture that inspires you. This is a good opportunity to select from organizations you know or your colleagues' organizations. What is their culture? How do their cultures align with their values?

_____
_____
_____
_____
_____

Sometimes it may seem as if you have no impact on organizational culture. You have an impact on the way you support the organization, your teammates, your manager, and clients. What can you do to impact the organization's culture in a way that inspires you?

_____
_____
_____
_____
_____

Question for Mentor: What corporate culture do you think exists in our organization or in your organization and how does that define your methods of success? How does it inspire you?

Reality Reveal

....
....
....
....
....
....

⫸ Activity 3: Navigating Corporate Politics

The navigation of corporate politics is essential for career success. This can be a challenging subject as corporate politics is a way that individuals or groups gain power, influence decisions, and achieve goals. Corporate politics exist at every level of the organization; however, the higher you rise organizationally, the more you will deal with corporate politics. That's a fact.

The benefits of understanding corporate politics within your organization is understanding the way things get done. What does it take to be promoted? What does it take to get the next big project? What does it take to get your projects, resources, and proposals approved?

Corporate politics can cause dysfunction. This can manifest in excessive competition, employee disengagement, favoritism, and even challenges and unethical behavior. Be watchful of these as they can lead to a toxic environment.

Navigation of corporate politics starts with observing the behavior of others and listening! Pay attention to how decisions are made, what information is needed, who holds what influence, and the dynamics of relationships within the organization. Cultivate relationships not only with those that you align with, but also those with different perspectives, so that you can understand their point of view.

Understand that there is an informal and formal structure to processes. Informal could be socializing the idea with others and understanding their level of support, points of view, or hesitations. Focus on results that align with the organization's mission and vision—not your personal goals. *Tip: Be creative, curious, and adaptive to the environment and be willing to give up if you do not have the support.*

Describe the corporate politics in your organization and your role as it appears to you.

....

....

....

What are the informal and formal processes to get decisions?

When you think of the processes to get new projects, promotions, invites to events, what does that look like in your organization? If you do not know, what steps would it take to understand these?

Who are the people of influence?

People of influence begin with your manager. How are they aligned in the organization? Who listens to them and who does not? How can you best support their initiatives so that they have more influence?

Who is aligned and who is not? What steps can you take to create collaboration and consensus?

Sometimes it is difficult to detect who is aligned and who is not. It may even be based on the subject. It is important to observe these dynamics to clue into what matters to each of your influencers.

....

....

....

Sometimes it may seem as if you have no impact on corporate politics. You have an impact on the way you navigate and support the organization, your teammates, your management, and clients. What can you do to impact the corporate politics in a way that inspires you?

....

....

....

Question: How does corporate politics affect what you do today? How you see corporate politics you evolve as you grew within organizations?

Reality Reveal

....

....

....

....

....

....

⟫ Activity 4: Allyships

Allyship, within the context of the workplace, is a deliberate and active commitment to fostering an inclusive environment by supporting and advocating for colleagues. It transcends mere awareness of diversity issues and involves taking tangible actions to create positive change. An ally is someone who not only acknowledges the challenges faced by individuals but actively works to dismantle systemic barriers and promote equity. In the workplace, allyship involves cultivating meaningful connections, demonstrating supportive behaviors, and fostering a heightened awareness of the experiences of others.

Building allyships is key to success whether it is with peers, your team, your boss, executives within your organization, your network, or your community. These allyships require time, open-mindedness, effort, and authenticity. A mentee can forge allyships by proactively participating in networking opportunities, attending events, and seeking out mentors and allies who align with their values.

Measuring the effectiveness of allyship relationships is crucial for sustained impact. This involves assessing both individual and collective awareness, behaviors, and connections. Regular check-ins and feedback sessions provide an opportunity for open communication, allowing mentees and allies to discuss their experiences, challenges, and areas for improvement. Tangible outcomes, such as increased collaboration, career advancement, and a more inclusive workplace culture, serve as indicators of the success of allyship relationships.

Ultimately, allies play a pivotal role in shaping organizational culture, driving innovation, and fostering a workplace where every individual feels valued and empowered to contribute their best.

When you think about the existing allyships you have today or relationships that you would like in the future, what are benefits of those relationships?

Reciprocal Support:

Allyship is a two-way street. Offer your support in areas where you excel or contribute your unique perspectives to projects. This creates a reciprocal dynamic, strengthening the allyship and fostering a collaborative environment.

Feedback and Adjustment:

Be open to feedback and be willing to adjust your approach based on the evolving dynamics of the relationship. This flexibility is key to ensuring the allyship remains beneficial and supportive for both parties.

Acknowledge and Appreciate:

Recognize and express gratitude for the support you receive. Acknowledge the positive impact your ally has on your professional growth and the overall work environment. Appreciation strengthens the bond and encourages continued support.

Expand Your Network:

While developing a primary ally is valuable, do not limit yourself. Cultivate relationships with a diverse group of colleagues who can provide varied perspectives and support. A broad network enhances your overall professional development.

Ultimately, allies play a pivotal role in shaping organizational culture, driving innovation, and fostering a workplace where every individual feels valued and empowered to contribute their best.

Remember, building allyships is an ongoing process that requires patience, authenticity, and a commitment to mutual growth. By taking these practical steps, you can lay the foundation for a supportive allyship within your organization.

Engaging in open and thoughtful conversations is crucial for building a successful mentoring relationship. Work with your mentor to identify potential allies within your organization or in your industry. Once you have identified potential allies, below are some questions you could ask a potential ally:

BACKGROUND AND EXPERIENCE:

Can you share a bit about your career journey and the experiences that have shaped your professional path?

_____
_____
_____
_____
_____
_____

How have you navigated challenges and setbacks in your career?

_____
_____
_____
_____
_____

ADVICE FOR CAREER DEVELOPMENT:

What advice do you have for someone at my career stage looking to advance professionally?

_____
_____
_____
_____
_____
_____

Are there specific skills or experiences you believe are crucial for success in our industry?

....

....

....

....

....

NAVIGATING THE ORGANIZATION:

How have you successfully navigated the organizational culture and dynamics?

....

....

....

....

....

....

Are there key stakeholders or unwritten rules I should be aware of as I progress in my career here?

....

....

....

....

....

....

BALANCING WORK AND LIFE:

How do you manage work-life balance, and are there strategies you have found effective in maintaining it?

_____
_____
_____
_____
_____

How have you handled moments of burnout or high-stress periods in your career?

_____
_____
_____
_____
_____

SETTING AND ACHIEVING GOALS:

How do you go about setting professional goals, and what strategies have helped you achieve them?

_____
_____
_____
_____
_____
_____

Can you share a specific example of a goal you set and accomplished in your career?

_____
_____
_____
_____
_____
_____
_____

FEEDBACK AND PROFESSIONAL GROWTH:

How do you actively seek and handle feedback in your role?

_____
_____
_____
_____
_____
_____

What are your strategies for continuous learning and professional development?

_____
_____
_____
_____
_____
_____
_____

BUILDING A PROFESSIONAL NETWORK:

How have you built and maintained your professional network throughout your career?

_____
_____
_____
_____
_____
_____

Are there specific networking opportunities or events you recommend for someone in my position?

_____
_____
_____
_____
_____
_____

DIVERSITY AND INCLUSION:

How do you see diversity and inclusion playing a role in career advancement within our organization?

_____
_____
_____
_____
_____

Are there initiatives or resources you recommend for someone interested in promoting diversity in the workplace?

....
....
....
....
....

Handling Challenges:

Can you share a challenging situation you faced in your career and how you overcame it?

....
....
....
....
....

What advice do you have for handling workplace conflicts or difficult conversations?

....
....
....
....
....

LEGACY AND IMPACT:

When you reflect on your career, what achievements or contributions are you most proud of?

....
....
....
....
....

How do you envision leaving a positive impact within the organization or industry?

....
....
....
....
....

These questions can serve as a starting point for meaningful discussions, helping you gain valuable insights and guidance from your potential ally. Adjusting the questions based on the specific context and goals of the mentoring relationship is encouraged to ensure relevance and depth in the conversations.

Now that you have some understanding of what an ally is and how it can be an inspiration, what steps can you take to become an ally? What would that look like? *Tip: Sometimes to find allies, you must be one first.*

....
....
....
....

Question for Mentor: How do you see allyship in your organization? How has it evolved over time? Where do you see opportunities?

Reality Reveal

....
....
....
....
....
....

⟫ Partnership Sunset and Final Calibration

The reason we call this sunset is that everything should have a beginning and end, but it does not have to be over. Look back on all that has been accomplished and provide gratitude for the time, effort, and wisdom from your mentor.

What are you grateful for from this experience?

_____
_____
_____
_____
_____

What part of this program have you enjoyed the most?

_____
_____
_____
_____

What part of this program have you enjoyed the least?

_____
_____
_____
_____
_____

Inspire To Aspire

How have you evolved as a professional?

How has this process inspired you?

What will you take away to inspire others?

How are you better prepared now for your future aspirations?

Part 3: Core Connections: Global View

What will it take for you to become a mentor?

How has your mentor shaped your views of yourself, your organization, and others?

How can you take what you have learned and share it with others?

If you had to do it all over again, what would you change?

Revisit your expectations, vision, and revised vision. What has changed and what has remained the same?

....

....

....

Set up a time in 2 to 3 months for a follow-up meeting. This allows you to review your 30/60/90-day plan that you committed to and where you review your wins and challenges with your mentor.

Create a plan for future connections:

....

....

....

....

Question for Mentor: What have you, the mentor, learned from me, the mentee?

Reality Reveal

....

....

....

....

....

....

Additional Resources

Proposed Timeline

The Proposed Timeline is a recommended timeline for the ultimate mentorship experience. This allows both you and your mentor to understand partnership commitment. The first four activities are designed for self-awareness and deep discovery and designed to be completed prior to your first meeting with your mentor.

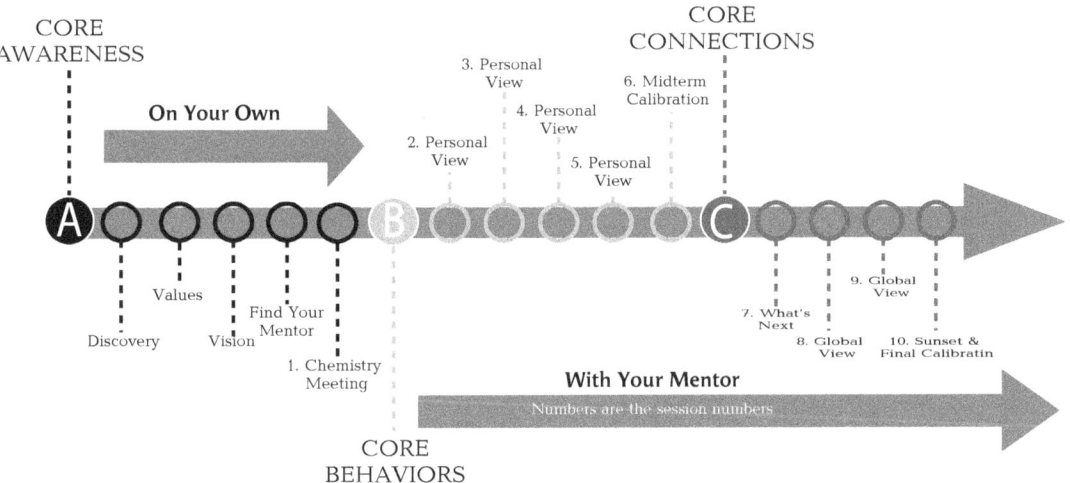

If you follow recommendations, this will be eight sessions with your mentor, not including mid-term and final assessment. If you choose to have these as separate sessions, this will include ten sessions with your mentor. If you meet every two weeks, this will take approximately five months.

Part 1: Core Awareness – Prepare for the Partnership

Activity 1: Discovery - Session 1 on your own

Activity 2: Core Values – Session 2 on your own

Activity 3: Personal Vision – Session 3 on your own

    Discovery Recap

Activity 4: Find Your Mentor? – Session 4 on your own

Activity 5: Chemistry Meeting – Session 1 with Mentor

PART 2: CORE BEHAVIORS – PERSONAL VIEW

(We recommend selecting 3-4 from activities that were your highest priority from discovery activity 1 in Core Awareness.) These will be Sessions 2-5 with your Mentor

Activity 1: Work and Home

Activity 2: Emotional Intelligence

Activity 3: Getting Out of Your Own Head

Activity 4: Goal Setting

Activity 5: Career Transition

Activity 6: Visibility and Influence

Activity 7: Confidence

Activity 8: Risk and Initiative

    Mid-term Calibration

    Reflect and What's Next

PART 3: CORE CONNECTIONS – GLOBAL VIEW AND PARTNERSHIP SUNSET
(Pick two from this section, sessions 6-7)

Activity 1: Networking

Activity 2: Organizational Culture

Activity 3: Navigating Corporate Politics

Activity 4: Allyships

    Partnership Sunset and Final Calibration

Mentorship Tracker 1

Use this tracker to prepare for your sessions with your mentor. This tracker will start from session 1, chemistry meeting with your mentor. You should complete this before your session and align homework expectations prior to session ending to ensure ultimate mentorship experience.

Get to Know Each Other

Favorite Food(s)?

Date: ....

PRIOR TO SESSION

What have I accomplished since our last session?

Between each session, you will have performed work either from this playbook or perhaps from assignments from your mentor. Take time to write this down prior to your session with your mentor so that you are prepared and they provide the best value to you.

....

....

....

What challenges am I facing right now?

Challenges could be from the homework, from situations arising in your work. How can your mentor help you? Perhaps they have experienced something similar and can provide guidance.

....

....

....

What opportunities are available to me right now?

This is an exciting time in your career and opportunities may arise that requires thought and reflection. Take the time to think about how this opportunity aligns with your aspirations and discuss this with your mentor.

....
....
....
....

Question for Mentor

In each section of this playbook, there is a posed question for your mentor. You can include that question here or another question from the homework. This could also be a question from your reality reveal that you would like insight on.

....
....
....
....

DURING SESSION:

What is the next topic that you and your mentor will work on for next session?

....
....

Additional Resources

Homework/Action Items

Each time you meet with your mentor, you should have a new section to perform or an article to read from your mentor or an action to take from the guidance of your mentor. Write that here and agree upon the homework and expectations for next session.

Mentorship Tracker 2

Use this tracker to prepare for your sessions with your mentor. You should complete this before your session and align homework expectations prior to session ending to ensure ultimate mentorship experience.

Date: ....

Get to Know Each Other

Most exotic place visited?

PRIOR TO SESSION

What have I accomplished since our last session?

Between each session, you will have performed work either from this playbook or perhaps from assignments from your mentor. Take time to write this down prior to your session with your mentor so that you are prepared and they provide the best value to you.

....

....

....

....

What challenges am I facing right now?

Challenges could be from the homework, from situations arising in your work. How can your mentor help you? Perhaps they have experienced something similar and can provide guidance.

....

....

Additional Resources

_____
_____
_____

What opportunities are available to me right now?

This is an exciting time in your career and opportunities may arise that requires thought and reflection. Take the time to think about how this opportunity aligns with your aspirations and discuss this with your mentor.

_____
_____
_____
_____
_____

Question for Mentor

In each section of this playbook, there is a posed question for your mentor. You can include that question here or another question from the homework. This could also be a question from your reality reveal that you would like insight on.

_____
_____
_____
_____
_____

DURING SESSION:

What is the next topic that you and your mentor will work on for next session?

....

....

....

....

HOMEWORK/ACTION ITEMS

Each time you meet with your mentor, you should have a new section to perform or an article to read from your mentor or an action to take from the guidance of your mentor. Write that here and agree upon the homework and expectations for next session.

....

....

....

....

....

Additional Resources

Mentorship Tracker 3

Use this tracker to prepare for your sessions with your mentor. You should complete this before your session and align homework expectations prior to session ending to ensure ultimate mentorship experience.

Date: ....

Get to Know Each Other

Describe your first job.

Prior to Session

What have I accomplished since our last session?

Between each session, you will have performed work either from this playbook or perhaps from assignments from your mentor. Take time to write this down prior to your session with your mentor so that you are prepared and they provide the best value to you.

_____

_____

_____

_____

What challenges am I facing right now?

Challenges could be from the homework, from situations arising in your work. How can your mentor help you? Perhaps they have experienced something similar and can provide guidance.

_____

_____

_____

What opportunities are available to me right now?

This is an exciting time in your career and opportunities may arise that requires thought and reflection. Take the time to think about how this opportunity aligns with your aspirations and discuss this with your mentor.

Question for Mentor

In each section of this playbook, there is a posed question for your mentor. You can include that question here or another question from the homework. This could also be a question from your reality reveal that you would like insight on.

Additional Resources

DURING SESSION:

What is the next topic that you and your mentor will work on for next session?

....

....

....

....

....

HOMEWORK/ACTION ITEMS

Each time you meet with your mentor, you should have a new section to perform or an article to read from your mentor or an action to take from the guidance of your mentor. Write that here and agree upon the homework and expectations for next session.

....

....

....

....

....

Mentorship Tracker 4

Use this tracker to prepare for your sessions with your mentor. You should complete this before your session and align with homework prior to session ending to ensure ultimate mentorship experience.

Date: ....

PRIOR TO SESSION

What have I accomplished since our last session?

Between each session, you will have performed work either from this playbook or perhaps from assignments from your mentor. Take time to write this down prior to your session with your mentor so that you are prepared and they provide the best value to you.

....
....
....
....

What challenges am I facing right now?

Challenges could be from the homework, from situations arising in your work. How can your mentor help you? Perhaps they have experienced something similar and can provide guidance.

....
....
....

Get to Know Each Other

Who was your worst boss? Describe characteristics.

Additional Resources

_____
_____
_____
_____

What opportunities are available to me right now?

This is an exciting time in your career and opportunities may arise that requires thought and reflection. Take the time to think about how this opportunity aligns with your aspirations and discuss this with your mentor.

_____
_____
_____
_____
_____

Question for Mentor

In each section of this playbook, there is a posed question for your mentor. You can include that question here or another question from the homework. This could also be a question from your reality reveal that you would like insight on.

_____
_____
_____
_____
_____

During Session:

What is the next topic that you and your mentor will work on for next session?

....

....

....

....

....

Homework/action items

Each time you meet with your mentor, you should have a new section to perform or an article to read from your mentor or an action to take from the guidance of your mentor. Write that here and agree upon the homework and expectations for next session.

....

....

....

....

....

Additional Resources

Mentorship Tracker 5

Use this tracker to prepare for your sessions with your mentor. You should complete this before your session and align with homework prior to session ending to ensure ultimate mentorship experience.

Date: ....

Prior to Session

What have I accomplished since our last session?

Between each session, you will have performed work either from this playbook or perhaps from assignments from your mentor. Take time to write this down prior to your session with your mentor so that you are prepared and they provide the best value to you.

....
....
....
....

What challenges am I facing right now?

Challenges could be from the homework, from situations arising in your work. How can your mentor help you? Perhaps they have experienced something similar and can provide guidance.

....
....

Get to Know Each Other

Who was your best boss? Describe characteristics.

What opportunities are available to me right now?

This is an exciting time in your career and opportunities may arise that requires thought and reflection. Take the time to think about how this opportunity aligns with your aspirations and discuss this with your mentor.

Question for Mentor

In each section of this playbook, there is a posed question for your mentor. You can include that question here or another question from the homework. This could also be a question from your reality reveal that you would like insight on.

Additional Resources

DURING SESSION:

What is the next topic that you and your mentor will work on for next session?

HOMEWORK/ACTION ITEMS

Each time you meet with your mentor, you should have a new section to perform or an article to read from your mentor or an action to take from the guidance of your mentor. Write that here and agree upon the homework and expectations for next session.

Mentorship Tracker 6

Use this tracker to prepare for your sessions with your mentor. You should complete this before your session and align with homework prior to session ending to ensure ultimate mentorship experience.

Get to Know Each Other

If you could invite anyone to dinner, who would it be and why?

Date: ....

PRIOR TO SESSION

What have I accomplished since our last session?

Between each session, you will have performed work either from this playbook or perhaps from assignments from your mentor. Take time to write this down prior to your session with your mentor so that you are prepared and they provide the best value to you.

....

....

....

....

What challenges am I facing right now?

Challenges could be from the homework, from situations arising in your work. How can your mentor help you? Perhaps they have experienced something similar and can provide guidance.

....

....

....

Additional Resources

What opportunities are available to me right now?

This is an exciting time in your career and opportunities may arise that requires thought and reflection. Take the time to think about how this opportunity aligns with your aspirations and discuss this with your mentor.

Question for Mentor

In each section of this playbook, there is a posed question for your mentor. You can include that question here or another question from the homework. This could also be a question from your reality reveal that you would like insight on.

During Session:

What is the next topic that you and your mentor will work on for next session?

....
....
....
....

Homework/action items

Each time you meet with your mentor, you should have a new section to perform or an article to read from your mentor or an action to take from the guidance of your mentor. Write that here and agree upon the homework and expectations for next session.

....
....
....
....
....

Mentorship Tracker 7

Use this tracker to prepare for your sessions with your mentor. You should complete this before your session and align with homework prior to session ending to ensure ultimate mentorship experience.

Get to Know Each Other

Favorite movie?

Date: ....

PRIOR TO SESSION

What have I accomplished since our last session?

Between each session, you will have performed work either from this playbook or perhaps from assignments from your mentor. Take time to write this down prior to your session with your mentor so that you are prepared and they provide the best value to you.

....
....
....
....

What challenges am I facing right now?

Challenges could be from the homework, from situations arising in your work. How can your mentor help you? Perhaps they have experienced something similar and can provide guidance.

....
....
....

What opportunities are available to me right now?

This is an exciting time in your career and opportunities may arise that requires thought and reflection. Take the time to think about how this opportunity aligns with your aspirations and discuss this with your mentor.

Question for Mentor

In each section of this playbook, there is a posed question for your mentor. You can include that question here or another question from the homework. This could also be a question from your reality reveal that you would like insight on.

During Session:

What is the next topic that you and your mentor will work on for next session?

....

....

....

....

Homework/action items

Each time you meet with your mentor, you should have a new section to perform or an article to read from your mentor or an action to take from the guidance of your mentor. Write that here and agree upon the homework and expectations for next session.

....

....

....

....

Mentorship Tracker 8

Use this tracker to prepare for your sessions with your mentor. You should complete this before your session and align with homework prior to session ending to ensure ultimate mentorship experience.

Date: ....

Get to Know Each Other

Favorite podcast or YouTube channel?

Prior to Session

What have I accomplished since our last session?

Between each session, you will have performed work either from this playbook or perhaps from assignments from your mentor. Take time to write this down prior to your session with your mentor so that you are prepared and they provide the best value to you.

....

....

....

....

What challenges am I facing right now?

Challenges could be from the homework, from situations arising in your work. How can your mentor help you? Perhaps they have experienced something similar and can provide guidance.

....

....

....

Additional Resources

What opportunities are available to me right now?

This is an exciting time in your career and opportunities may arise that requires thought and reflection. Take the time to think about how this opportunity aligns with your aspirations and discuss this with your mentor.

Question for Mentor

In each section of this playbook, there is a posed question for your mentor. You can include that question here or another question from the homework. This could also be a question from your reality reveal that you would like insight on.

DURING SESSION:

What is the next topic that you and your mentor will work on for next session?

....
....
....
....
....

HOMEWORK/ACTION ITEMS

Each time you meet with your mentor, you should have a new section to perform or an article to read from your mentor or an action to take from the guidance of your mentor. Write that here and agree upon the homework and expectations for next session.

....
....
....
....
....

Mentorship Tracker 9

Use this tracker to prepare for your sessions with your mentor. You should complete this before your session and align with homework prior to session ending to ensure ultimate mentorship experience.

Get to Know Each Other

Do for fun?

Date: ....

PRIOR TO SESSION

What have I accomplished since our last session?

Between each session, you will have performed work either from this playbook or perhaps from assignments from your mentor. Take time to write this down prior to your session with your mentor so that you are prepared and they provide the best value to you.

....
....
....
....

What challenges am I facing right now?

Challenges could be from the homework, from situations arising in your work. How can your mentor help you? Perhaps they have experienced something similar and can provide guidance.

....
....
....

What opportunities are available to me right now?

This is an exciting time in your career and opportunities may arise that requires thought and reflection. Take the time to think about how this opportunity aligns with your aspirations and discuss this with your mentor.

Question for Mentor

In each section of this playbook, there is a posed question for your mentor. You can include that question here or another question from the homework. This could also be a question from your reality reveal that you would like insight on.

Additional Resources

DURING SESSION:

What is the next topic that you and your mentor will work on for next session?

....
....
....
....
....

HOMEWORK/ACTION ITEMS

Each time you meet with your mentor, you should have a new section to perform or an article to read from your mentor or an action to take from the guidance of your mentor. Write that here and agree upon the homework and expectations for next session.

....
....
....
....
....

Mentorship Tracker 10

Use this tracker to prepare for your sessions with your mentor. You should complete this before your session and align with homework prior to session ending to ensure ultimate mentorship experience.

Date: ....

Prior to Session

What have I accomplished since our last session?

Between each session, you will have performed work either from this playbook or perhaps from assignments from your mentor. Take time to write this down prior to your session with your mentor so that you are prepared and they provide the best value to you.

....
....
....
....

What challenges am I facing right now?

Challenges could be from the homework, from situations arising in your work. How can your mentor help you? Perhaps they have experienced something similar and can provide guidance.

....
....
....

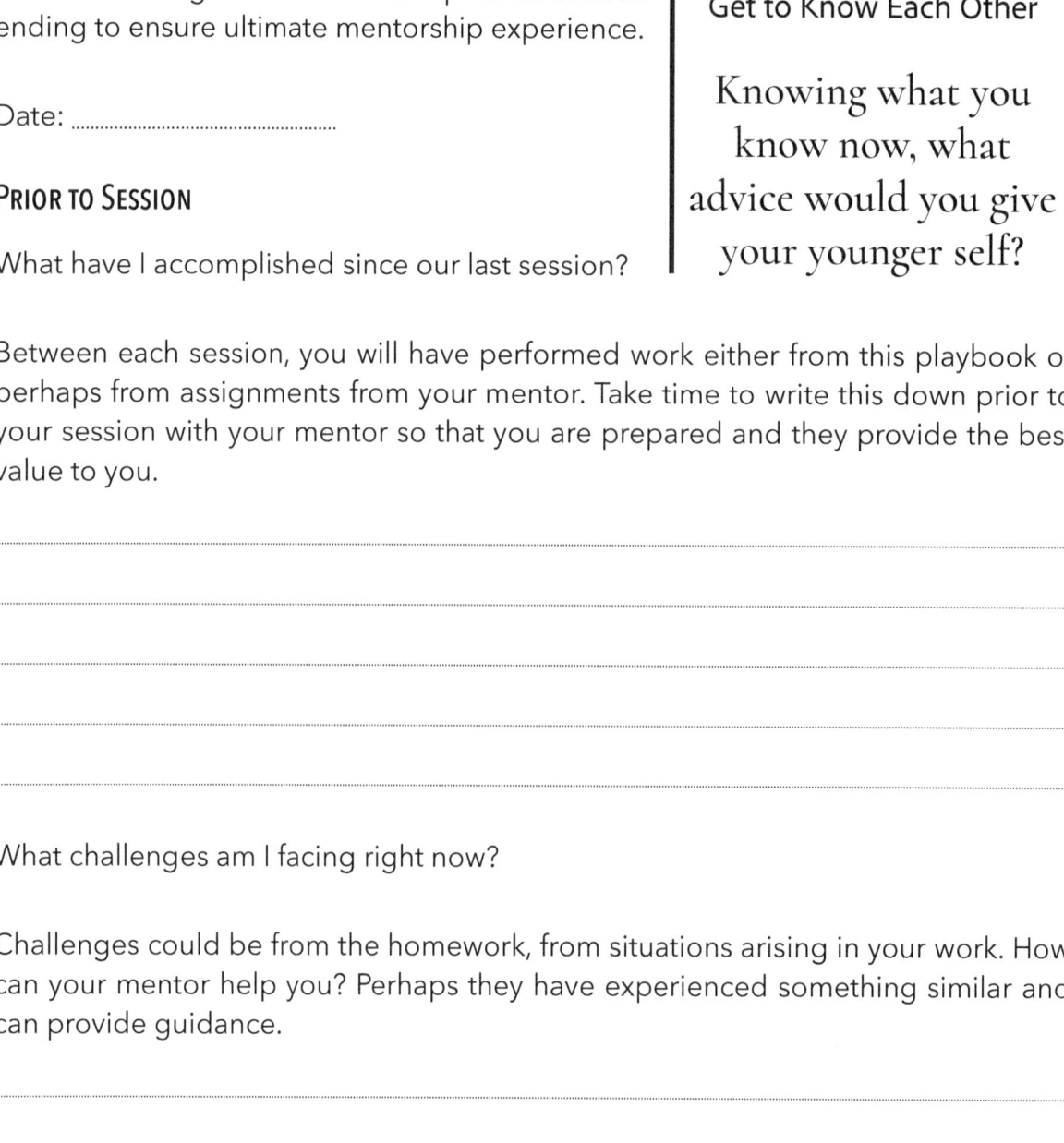

Get to Know Each Other

Knowing what you know now, what advice would you give your younger self?

Additional Resources

What opportunities are available to me right now?

This is an exciting time in your career and opportunities may arise that requires thought and reflection. Take the time to think about how this opportunity aligns with your aspirations and discuss this with your mentor.

Question for Mentor

In each section of this playbook, there is a posed question for your mentor. You can include that question here or another question from the homework. This could also be a question from your reality reveal that you would like insight on.

During Session:

What is the next topic that you and your mentor will work on for next session?

....
....
....
....

Homework/action items

Each time you meet with your mentor, you should have a new section to perform or an article to read from your mentor or an action to take from the guidance of your mentor. Write that here and agree upon the homework and expectations for next session.

....
....
....
....

Meet the Authors

JENNIFER CHLOUPEK, M.ED. is a world-renowned Master Executive Coach, facilitator, and author. She is the co-author of numerous books that are taught internationally both in the public and private sector. Chloupek has over 25 years of experience as an educator, strategic planner, and leader. Jenn has worked with many Fortune 500 companies as well as Federal Agencies. She is the Co-Founder and CEO of Chloupek Consulting Services. Her mission is to connect people to their true identity, to tools and resources, and to other people in order to champion human potential. She lives in Arizona with her husband, Lar.

MICHELLE ESTADES JACK is a dynamic architect of success, drawing from extensive experiences in spearheading transformative journeys for organizations, teams, and individuals. Armed with an undergraduate degree in Business from the University of Texas at Austin and a masters in Human Dimensions of Organizations from the same institution, Michelle brings a powerful blend of academic prowess and real-world acumen. Her executive coaching certification from the University of Georgia further amplifies her expertise.

A trailblazing visionary and accomplished author, Michelle passionately champions a guided process that marries self-awareness, practical applications, and success tips. She doesn't just inspire; she propels her readers into a realm where inspiration seamlessly intertwines with actionable strategies, creating the ultimate environment for unparalleled success. Michelle Estades Jack is not just an author; she is your compass on the exhilarating journey to triumph.

www.ingramcontent.com/pod-product-compliance
Lightning Source LLC
Chambersburg PA
CBHW060233240426
43671CB00016B/2931